GW00746070

The Expr
The Woman's Guic

Third edit.

Tony Levene

"covers everything from the cost of having a baby to retirement"
Cosmopolitan

"this non-technical book is a good, primary source of enlightenment"
Scotland on Sunday

"an excellent and very informative book"
Abbey National

"packed with practical and reliable advice on every aspect of money management from a woman's perspective"
Portsmouth News

Winner of an Abbey National's Golden Pen Award for the best personal finance book of the year.

Whether you are a single career woman or a mother bringing up children, *The Woman's Guide to Finance* will show you how to take control of all aspects of your finances. Topics covered include:

- savings strategies
- choosing the best savings account
- tax matters
- money and marriage
- maternity rights
- pensions
- widowhood
- giving to charity

and many more.

Written in a down-to-earth and readable style, this completely revised and updated edition, shows women the importance of financial planning for a more prosperous future.

Tony Levene is a financial journalist with over 20 years' experience. Specializing in family money matters, he writes for national newspapers and has written five other books.

The Express Guides

A series of practical guides offering no-nonsense advice on a wide range of financial, legal and business topics.

Whether you want to manage your money better, make more money, get a new business idea off the ground – and make sure it's legal – there's an Express Guide for you.

Titles published so far are:

Great Ideas for Making Money
Niki Chesworth

Your Money
How to Make the Most of it
Niki Chesworth

Buying a Property Abroad
Niki Chesworth

How to Sell More
Neil Johnson

The Woman's Guide to Finance
Tony Levene

Buying Your First Franchise
G R Clarke

The Daily Express Investment Guide
Tony Levene

Network Marketing
David Barber

How to Cope with Separation and Divorce
David Green

Your Home Office
Peter Chatterton

You and the Law
A Simple Guide to All Your Legal Problems
Susan Singleton

How to Cut Your Tax Bill Without Breaking the Law
Grant Thornton, Chartered Accountants

Be Your Own Boss!
How to Set Up a Successful Small Business
David McMullan

Readymade Business Letters That Get Results
Jim Douglas

Self Assessment for the Small Business and the Self-Employed
Niki Chesworth

Available from all good bookshops, or to obtain further information please contact the publishers at the address below:

Kogan Page Ltd
120 Pentonville Rd
LONDON N1 9JN
Tel: 0171-278 0433
Fax: 0171-837 6348

THE EXPRESS

THE WOMAN'S GUIDE TO FINANCE

How to Manage all your Money Matters

Third Edition

Tony Levene

KOGAN
PAGE

First published in 1995

Second edition 1997

This edition published in 1998

Kogan Page Limited
120 Pentonville Road
London N1 9JN

© Tony Levene 1995, 1997, 1998

British Library Cataloguing in Publication Data
A CIP record for this book is available from the British Library.

ISBN 0 7494 2766 3

Typeset by Saxon Graphics Ltd, Derby
Printed in Great Britain by Bell and Bain Ltd., Glasgow

Contents

PERSONA.
CONTRACEPTION **FOR PEOPLE WHO DON'T LIKE** CONTRACEPTIVES.

You need contraception but you don't like using contraceptives. With PERSONA you don't have to.

Because, you see, most days of the month you can't get pregnant so you don't need contraceptives. But you do need to know when these days are.

PERSONA, a method of contraception that works with your body, tells you this by measuring your hormones.

PERSONA builds up a picture of your cycle through a series of simple urine tests at key times of the month so you'll know when you are free to make love without contraceptives.

PERSONA has been tested in independent home trials across Europe; it's 94%* reliable when used according to instructions and as the only method of contraception.

For more information talk to your pharmacist or doctor. Alternatively call 0345 44 77 44 for an information booklet. PERSONA is available at leading pharmacies.

Contraception in harmony with your body. **PERSONA**

*A reliability rate of 94% means that if 100 women use PERSONA for 1 year, 6 would be expected to become pregnant as a result of PERSONA incorrectly identifying the fertile phase. The reliability figures apply if PERSONA is used according to instructions and as your only method of contraception. PERSONA does not protect against HIV and other STIs. PERSONA trademark is owned by Unipath Ltd. Bedford.
www.unipath.com/persona2

Simplicity and choice from Ford Credit

Ford Credit changes the face of finance!

Ford Credit announce the launch of 'Optimise' - a new solution that lets you decide the best way to pay for your new or used car.

When you buy a car from your Ford Dealer, the first choice you make, naturally enough, is to decide on the car you want.

But there's another decision that's worth taking just as seriously - what's the best way to pay for it?

Today there are lots of choices confronting car buyers. Some are easy to understand - but others can appear complicated - and even intimidating. So despite having more choice than ever, deciding which method is right for you can be far from straightforward.

What is Optimise?

Optimise is the range of financial alternatives available from Ford Credit. When you visit your Ford Dealer, you will find an Optimise brochure on display containing details of all Ford Credit finance plans. The brochure will act as a guide to help you make an informed decision on the best way to finance your car.

"As Ford's own bank. Ford Credit is dedicated to helping customers drive the car they really want" commented Phil Hollins, Director of Marketing. "Optimise has been designed to make the process of buying a car and deciding how to pay for it more straightforward and convenient. It puts the customer in control and gives them confidence to find the right finance plan to suit their individual needs."

What does Optimise really mean for you?

Simplicity...   Optimise cuts out unnecessary jargon and clearly
explains your financial alternatives.

Flexibility...   To decide how much - or how little - deposit you wish to pay and spread your payments over any period between 12 and 48 months to fit your budget.

Choice...   Select from a range of Optimise financial alternatives to
find the best plan for you.

Experience the 'One Stop Shop'...

...at one of over 800 Ford Dealerships in the UK. Most Ford Dealers are open 7 days a week with convenient opening hours to suit today's busy lifestyle. Usually there's no need to make an appointment and you should be able to find a parking space!

You can choose the car you want and arrange how to pay for it under one roof - quickly and easily - using the latest Ford technology.

Also, to make life easier, most Ford Dealerships have trained Finance Specialists to guide you through the details. He or she has undergone comprehensive training conducted by Ford Credit and is qualified to offer objective advice on the best way to finance your new or used car.

Who knows... with the range of financial alternatives available through Optimise, you may even be able to afford a better car than you thought possible...!

Ford Credit - and Optimise............
............Your first choice for finance

Lo Call: 0345 346 347
www.fordcredit.co.uk

Finance subject to status. Guarantees and indemnities may be required.
Written quotations; FREEPOST FCE Bank plc.

Introduction

No woman can afford to ignore the subject of finance

Why write — and more importantly why read — a book about money for women? Surely the days when a married woman's property became that of her husband; when she needed his permission to open a bank account; and when her taxation affairs were so joined with his that she could be better off living together unmarried, are long gone?

They have all disappeared although separate taxation for married women was only introduced as late as 1990. More than half of all women now work outside the home; and it is rare to find a woman who still hands over all her savings and earnings to her spouse. And in any case, it is argued, money is sex blind. Whether you are a woman or a man, you will get the same return on your cash if you invest it identically.

Despite all these advances, a woman's finances are not like those of a man. This has nothing to do with emotions or feelings: it is a hard fact. And because of that, it is equally valid for a man to write this book.

For a start, the insurance companies are specifically exempt from sex discrimination legislation. They can set different rates for females and males. This can work both for and against women. Women tend to enjoy lower motor insurance as they are deemed 'safer' (although lower mileage may have something to do with it).

The fact that women live approximately six years longer than men means they benefit from lower life insurance premiums. A 39-year-old woman who does not smoke can buy £100,000 of life cover for the next 20 years for £36 a month with one leading life insurer. Her male counterpart would pay £46 a month.

On the minus side, insurers claim that women are ill more often than men 'according to their records'. They translate this into a 50 per cent extra charge on premiums for permanent health insurance — a policy which pays out if you cannot work through illness for longer than a set period which can range from a month to a year. Insurance companies ignore the argument that women do not suffer any more long-term illness than men. They rely on their own records — and as very few women can afford to buy this cover at the high price they are charging, many companies do not have much in the way of statistics on which to base their premium increase.

And women get a bad deal on pensions as the chapters on retirement planning clearly show. The ideal person, from the point of view of the pensions industry, spends 40 years working with one company without a break. Time off for children or looking after elderly parents? Forget it — or if the scheme allows it, expect to pay a cost penalty for the privilege.

Which sex has to suffer from the move to equal state pension age? Men will stay at 65; but women born after 1955 will find their pension age goes up from the present 60 to 65. And even when women are allowed to retire, they will probably end up with less than men thanks to generally lower earnings and career breaks.

Personal pensions also discriminate against women. A woman who has built up a £100,000 personal pension at 65 will have a monthly income of £803 from one top pension provider. Her male counterpart gets £820 with a top company — the gap can be wider. The excuse of this and other insurers? Women live longer so the money has to be spread more thinly.

It took emergency action through Parliament to force one building society converting to public company status to give a bonus payment to 5000 widows who were — because of sexism — the second named after their late husbands on the savings books for joint accounts. The Cheltenham & Gloucester argued that the law as it then stood meant that a payout could only be made to a member and that the member was always

the first named. The law may officially ignore the female/male divide but hastily drafted legislation can all too often end up discriminating against half the population.

All this is before the 'lifestyle' difficulties. Single parenthood, divorce and widowhood all affect women far more than men. There is still no agreement on how to split pensions after a divorce even though they can represent as asset as great as the roof over your head.

And women in relationships are still treated differently by different government departments. The Inland Revenue considers you as married for tax purposes including the Married Couple's Allowance only if you hold a legal marriage certificate. The Department of Social Security treats both married women and those with a partner — 'cohabitees' in DSS jargon — as the same. A single mother, without an income of her own, living with a partner is deemed to be dependent on his finances by the DSS whatever the reality of the situation.

So, the main theme of this book is the importance of financial independence, whether you are a single career woman or a mother with children.

Being in control of your finances brings you confidence and freedom. It means you can look forward to a more prosperous future.

And it means you — and your children — are less financially vulnerable if a crisis, such as divorce or separation, happens.

This book aims to give financial planning advice for women taking into account those life changes. However, it is intended to be a springboard for women who want to learn the basics, not as an exhaustive manual. Details of where to get further information and help are included at the end of each chapter.

Take to the road with Optimise

Deciding on the best way to finance your car is as important as choosing the car itself. So it pays to get it right.

Simply answer the questions on the Optimise Route Planner and discover which plan is right for you. Then, simply talk to your Ford Dealer.

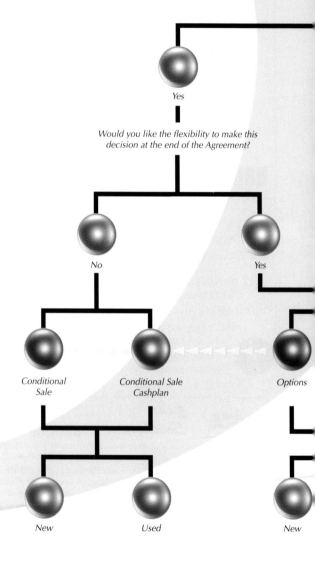

Yes

Would you like the flexibility to make this decision at the end of the Agreement?

No

Yes

Conditional Sale

Conditional Sale Cashplan

Options

New

Used

New

The best route for car finance

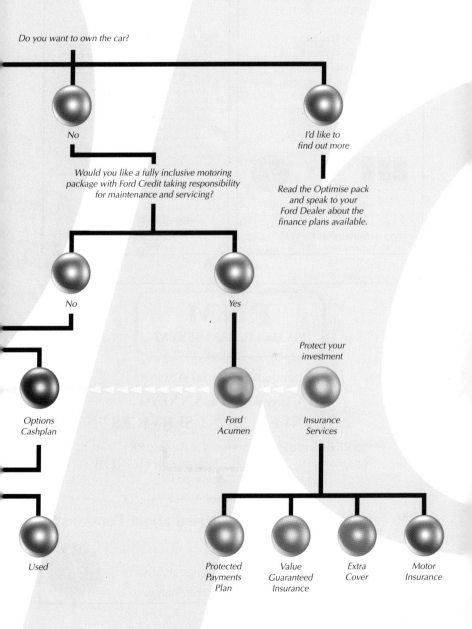

Do you want to own the car?

No

I'd like to
find out more

Would you like a fully inclusive motoring
package with Ford Credit taking responsibility
for maintenance and servicing?

Read the Optimise pack
and speak to your
Ford Dealer about the
finance plans available.

No

Yes

Protect your
investment

Options
Cashplan

Ford
Acumen

Insurance
Services

Used

Protected
Payments
Plan

Value
Guaranteed
Insurance

Extra
Cover

Motor
Insurance

1

Savings strategies

Most women aim to save both for short-term peace of mind and to build up longer-term capital. There are thousands of savings products available — the only problem is choosing the one best suited to your needs. In the past, women did not enjoy full independence when it came to savings. Married women were forced to reveal their savings to their husbands as men were responsible for tax returns. Fortunately, that unfair situation ended in 1990, giving women complete privacy regarding their savings, however large or small.

Your savings aims

What are you saving for? Which type of savings plan is the best option depends on your aims, how long you want to save for, whether you might need to get your hands on the money in a hurry, and how much risk you are prepared to take.

All women should, however, consider three priorities.

- *Emergency funds*: It's well worth trying to build up a pot of emergency cash in a bank or building society account where you can get it at short notice, in case you suddenly find yourself faced with a big repair bill for your car or your home, for example. This should be in your name alone. You never know, in an emotional emergency, it could be your 'running away' money.
- *Protect your family*: Make sure you have sufficient life insurance to provide for your dependants should anything happen. Remember that mums who stay at home to look after the family need insuring too — according to one insurance company, it would cost around £18,000 to buy in the clean-

ing, cooking and childcare and other services a mother provides each year. So few families could substitute you with a paid replacement.

Check that you have house buildings and contents cover and car insurance — it's a false economy to go without the first two and illegal to ignore the third.

- *Planning for retirement*: Women need independent pensions but not all qualify. This is covered in more detail in the chapters on pensions later in the book.

  Women should also consider:

- *Short-term savings*: Short-term savings goals are aims you want to achieve within one or two years, such as a holiday, a new car, or even an expensive designer outfit. Here, your priority is to get the best return without locking your money in an account with heavy notice penalties. Stick to safe savings accounts like bank and building society accounts. And don't forget the new supermarket banks which have some of the best rates around, although whether they will always be market leaders is less certain.

- *Medium term savings*: This is money you are setting aside for up to five years, and which you won't need in a hurry. Here, you can consider a range of tax-efficient accounts from banks, building societies and National Savings that are designed for savers who can tie their money up for five years. You will also be able to get better rates of return by putting your money into notice accounts. But remember that this does mean paying a penalty if you do take your money out before time.

- *Long-term savings*: This is money you can set aside for more than five years, for instance to finance a child's higher education, or to boost your retirement income. Here, you could consider savings linked to the stock market, which over time should provide a better return than the building society. Possibilities include PEPs, unit trusts and investment trusts, along with friendly society plans and endowment policies.

A compelling tale of sex, work and a decent pension.

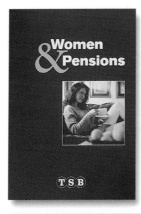

Our guide contains more surprises than a Whodunit.

Did you know that half the country's women are likely to suffer financial hardship when they retire?

To make the most of your retirement, order our free guide today.

It could be the most important thing you read this year.

Call TSB PhoneBank now for your free guide quoting ref: WF **0645 758 700** Ⓣ Ⓢ Ⓑ

Yes, I would like to receive my FREE guide, 'Women & Pensions' from TSB.

Surname: (Mr/Mrs/Miss/Ms)..................................First Name: ....

Address:..

...

Postcode:..Telephone No: ....

We'd like to contact you from time to time with details about services from TSB and other TSB Group companies if we think they'd interest you.

However, if you'd prefer not to be told about these services, please tick this box ☐.

TSB PhoneBank may call you to check you have received your guide, and if you have any questions, arrange a time for you to see one of our advisers.

Send to: TSB PhoneBank, FREEPOST (BM6334), Glasgow G2 8BR.

WF

Risk and reward

The more risk you are prepared to take with your savings, the greater the potential for reward. Although putting your money in the bank or building society is normally thought of as a safe investment, over the long term the buying power of your nest-egg is at risk from inflation. If you put £1000 in the building society now and spend the interest, you will still have £1000 capital in 20 years' time. But suppose prices rise at 5 per cent a year. Your £1000 will only be worth the equivalent of £377.

Research suggests women are more risk averse than men when it comes to investments. Fewer than one in ten women own unit trusts or stocks and shares. But this is likely to change as more women realise that long-term investments linked to the stock market stand a good chance of keeping up with inflation and of doing better than the bank or the building society. Over time, stock market investments can provide you with good capital growth and a rising income.

The disadvantage is that you have less security. With share-based investments like unit or investment trusts, the value of your capital can go down as well as up. Other options are endowment policies or friendly society plans, which smooth out the ups and downs of the stock market.

If you do want to put some cash into a riskier investment, always keep at least some of your money in a safe haven as a back-up. Investments linked to the stock market are most suitable for money you don't expect to need for five years or more. Always be sure to spread the risks around. And never forget that if a scheme looks too good to be true, then it is!

How do you want to save?

Most savings accounts will accept a lump sum investment. If you are lucky enough to have come into a large windfall it's best to take independent financial advice on how to invest it. Saving regularly is a good habit to get into. It's a sensible idea to set up a standing order to your savings account — that way the money is paid in automatically, so you won't be tempted to break good resolutions and buy a new dress instead.

Some longer-term investments, including friendly society plans and endowment policies, are specially designed for regular savers and have financial penalties if you fail to keep up your payments. Others, including unit and investment trusts, have regular savings options, which do not penalise you if you stop the plan.

Do you need an income now?

Most working women don't need to take an income from their savings immediately. They can reinvest the interest or dividends they earn so it is added to their capital. But if you have retired, you probably rely on your savings to boost your income.

Bank and building society variable savings rates go up and down in line with interest rates in the economy.

Alternatively, you can opt for a fixed rate investment, where the interest you get is guaranteed for a given period. These include gilts, and bank and building society fixed rate accounts. Buying a fixed rate investment is a gamble — if interest rates rise, you may lose out. Equally, you may do better! No one can really foretell the next week in the investment world.

Stockmarket investments offer the potential of a rising income over time, though the dividends paid out may fall as well as rise.

Be sceptical of any product offering an income that seems too good to be true — because it probably is. Many so-called 'high income' investments are not really paying a high income at all — they are simply returning part of your capital. Other schemes based on anything from ostrich breeding to 'computerised' share picking may be fraudulent.

Making the most of savings

Do you keep a check of your savings — and how much they earn? Millions are lost each year because savers leave their money in 'dead' savings accounts. Banks and building societies often close down accounts to new investors in order to promote newer savings products paying tempting rates. When that happens, unsuspecting savers can be left earning very poor rates of interest — sometimes less than 1 per cent. Check with your bank or building society that you are not in an obsolete account, or switch to one which makes a commitment not to short-change savers.

Make sure you channel some of your longer-term money into tax-free investments such as friendly society plans, TESSAs, PEPs — both of which are to be replaced by the Individual Savings Account in April 1999 — and National Savings Certificates. The Inland Revenue deducts 20 per cent automatically from most other savings income. But there are tax-breaks for non-taxpayers. Women who don't work outside the home and other non-taxpayers should apply to receive their bank and building society interest without tax deducted — ask about form R85.

Married couples can save tax by switching investments into the name of the lower earning partner — see the chapters on tax and on money and marriage for more details. But high-achieving career wives should bear in mind that any transfers have to be outright gifts — although, as with any gift, it can always be returned. For low and non-earners, this is not a problem.

Flexibility for life

On average, you are likely to change your job every five years – and you may take breaks to raise a family, retrain, or because of redundancy, illness or accident.

Do you know what you are doing tomorrow?

Next week? Next year?

Lincoln has launched a pension designed to provide security for your future and flexibility for your lifestyle today – whatever your job, whatever your circumstances.

In short, a pension that provides flexibility for life.

Find out how a Lincoln pension offers security and flexibility for you, to meet your changing lifestyle and unpredictable future. Contact freephone **0800 7319635** quoting reference FPW – to find out more.

Lincoln is a marketing group regulated by the Personal Investment Authority providing life assurance, pensions and unit trusts.

001208 - 4/98

A member of Lincoln Financial Group

GIRLS ON TOP

Working women cherish being able to afford life's little luxuries - the Greek getaway once a year or the odd night out with friends, makes it all worthwhile. While women make up just over half of the overall population, 51% (1), they also constitute just under half the employed population, and the time is only around the corner when working women will outnumber working men.

Having a job and a salary is not just about greater independence - it's about more choice. Whether you like it or not, money matters, and more money means having freedom to do what you want to do.

But it takes more than a weekly wage to really go it alone and it's only by carefully organising your finances that you gain greater control over your life. More and more women are taking responsibility for their financial affairs, and are becoming more sophisticated in the financial products they are taking out.

So what does all this mean for you?

It means that, as you no longer have to rely on your partner for housekeeping money, neither should you rely on him to secure your financial future.

Lincoln believes everyone now has the purchasing power to buy whatever financial products suit their needs, whether it's saving for a rainy day, investing for your future or protecting your mortgage, there is something out there for you.

'Financial Planning' covers a whole host of things and certainly isn't as boring as it sounds. Consider it as a way of enabling you to afford to buy what you want to buy and of protecting what's important to you.

It's a fact of life that women need to pay more attention to their finances than men, because they are more likely to work part-time, and take career breaks to start a family. They also receive lower pensions in retirement than men, around one-tenth lower, because they live longer and tend to retire earlier.

There are certain areas where women need to pay particular attention, so here are some tips from Lincoln to make sure you stay on top:

Pensions

Women need to lavish special care on their pension because, with one in three marriages ending in divorce, (an estimated 174,000 couples untied the knot in 1996), more often than not a pension will be all they have to rely on for income in retirement.

Encouragingly, whilst around 9 million working men have some sort of pension provision, there are nearly 6 million women who belong either to an occupational scheme or who have taken out their own pension plan. (2) Yet, considering there are just under 11 million women in employment, (2) this still means that nearly half have no pension provision at all, and this is a situation that women must address.

Every woman should have some sort of pension over and above what the state provides and there are a number of reasons why this is the case:

First and foremost, everyone receives attractive tax breaks when they take out a pension. For every £1 you or your employer contributes, the government will pay in a further 23p or 40p on your behalf, depending on what level tax payer you are.

Secondly, if you don't have your own form of pension provision, you're not going to receive very much by way of income when you retire - it's as simple as that. The basic state pension is just over £62 a week (almost £65 a week from April 1998) for a single person and just under £100 a week (just over £103 from April 1998) for a married couple - could you live comfortably on that?

The amount you will receive from the state top up pension (SERPS) will depend on the number of national insurance contributions you have made. This means that a lot of women who work part time may not clock up enough earnings to qualify for SERPS pay out. To make matters worse, part-timers may not have put in enough hours on the time sheet to qualify for even their company pension scheme.

Women working part-time shouldn't neglect their pension provision. Even if you are not paying tax on your earnings you can still contribute net of basic rate income tax into a personal pension. Remember, retirement is a full-time occupation!

Thirdly, unless you are working you can't pay into a pension. If you take time off to have children you will make a big dent in the size of your pension pot, which will reduce the income you receive when you eventually retire.

For example, a 27 year-old woman paying £100 a month into her personal pension plan, taking four years off to have a child, could reduce her eventual pension by up to £3000 a year. More practically, if you have grown accustomed to two salaries, it will be a dramatic drop if you suddenly have to survive on just one pension when you both retire.

If you are lucky enough to work for a company which provides an employee pension scheme, then join it - in many cases your employer will be paying money into it for you. If it is a final salary scheme, this may be a considerable amount. Consider making additional contributions into it if you can, these will help to boost your benefits.

If your company does not provide a pension or you are self-employed, the next best thing is to take out a personal pension and pay into it on your own. The sooner you start to pay in as much as you can comfortably afford, the better.

Women in particular need flexibility when it comes to choosing a pension. Lincoln recommend that you choose one which allows you to stop payments without penalty if you decide to take a career break or have children, and one which will allow you to reduce payments, if, for example, you decide to return to work part-time. Most importantly it is vital to choose a pension that not only suits you today, but which offers you flexibility for life.

Protection

The word protection is often used to describe life and health insurance because that is exactly what these policies offer - they will protect your family's standard of living in the face of life's crises and will pay you a lump sum of money or a regular income to help you cope.

Life Assurance

While most people understand the need for life cover to enable them to pay off their mortgage if either partner dies, fewer people stop to consider how they are going to pay all of the bills on just one salary.

As a general rule of thumb, a married couple should

insure their lives for around ten times their combined annual salary, so that if one dies and the other is literally left 'holding the baby' the surviving partner has enough money left over to cope after repaying the mortgage. This is particularly true of women with young families where the cost of a child minder can often outweigh the benefit of going to work. Even where the woman has a low income - or no income at all - you should still be insured to help your partner cope with the children and bills if anything should happen to you.

Health Insurance

Whilst life assurance pays out if you die, there are various health insurance policies which will help you cope if you fall seriously ill, have an accident or become disabled. They fall into two main categories: those that pay a lump sum and those that replace most of your income until you retire if you are unable to ever work again. Lincoln say this is not as unlikely as you may think. At any one time there are over 1.5 million people registered as totally incapacitated by sickness or injury who have to rely on state benefits.

Critical Illness, Permanent Health Insurance and Accident, Sickness and Unemployment insurance are all valuable protection schemes which will keep your finances healthy even when you're not. Lincoln encourages all individuals, families, parents etc. to take out these types of insurance as they are the foundations of a happy lifestyle, and in the event that anything should happen you will still be able to manage.

Savings and Investment

Out of all the financial products which are available, savings products are one of the most easy to understand and most commonly taken out.

We're all familiar with the concept of saving, either in a bank or building society account, but fewer feel comfortable with shopping around for the best deal.

Whether you are saving on a regular basis or have a lump sum to make the most of, it always pays to look for the best rate with the minimum of hassle. The difference between instant access accounts can be as much as 5%. (3)

If you are willing to tie your money up for longer, then you can benefit from a higher rate of income and if you are prepared to take that little extra risk you may be rewarded even more.

With-profit, investment and guaranteed bonds are all ways of potentially beating building society returns whilst capping the amount of risk you are taking with your original capital investment.

Mortgages

At last, the UK's mortgage market has finally woken up to the needs of women and now offers a range of flexible mortgages to more appropriately reflect women's changing lifestyles.

Some mortgages now offer repayment 'holidays' to make it easier for periods where women stop working to have a family and the family is reduced to a single income for a short time. This makes it easier to budget at a time when there are additional costs of children to consider.

There are even one or two 'baby' mortgages now available which will allow you to borrow back some of the money you have repaid to help cover the costs of the new addition to the family.

More recently there are 'savings' mortgages which will allow you to overpay your mortgage on either a regular or lump sum basis. The pot of money you build up will earn the same rate of interest as you pay on your loan and the money can be accessed at any time in case of emergency.

Tax

Finally, all women, married and single, are now taxed as individuals and have their own tax allowance. At the moment, everyone can earn £4,045 a year without paying tax but when a couple marry they qualify for an additional married couple's allowance of £1,830 a year, this is still valuable even though it now only attracts tax relief at 15%. This is automatically added to the husband's allowance, although if you are working and your husband is not you may ask the tax man to transfer the allowance to you to lower the amount of tax you pay.

If money is the real key to independence then it is encouraging that women have more freedom than ever before. It now seems incredible that in the not too distant past, in some occupations, women who married were made to forfeit their jobs for the benefit of single women, because they had their husbands to provide for them!

In the 1990s, the decade which saw the introduction of the 'househusband', such a thing could simply not happen. In order to maintain their long-fought and hard-won individuality, women now need to safeguard, insure and protect their financial independence.

> Women have fought long and hard for political equality. Now it's time to seize control of your money matters too, says Louise Webber of Lincoln. Today, thankfully, you don't have to be a suffragette to prove your financial independence; simply taking out your own pension or opening a savings account will do!

The insurance industry has and is changing. It now recognises the need to address its audience on an individual basis, without the use of technical jargon. You can also be sure that all financial advisers are now trained to professional standards. So don't be put off.

Lincoln recommends that you find an adviser who is keen to provide you with the information that you need in order to make the choices you feel best address your priorities. Whether you choose an independent adviser or one from a company sales force, both are required to give 'best advice', only the finer details of the products may differ.

It is never too early or too late to improve your finances, so you can have the lifestyle you want and the ability to maintain it.

1) *NOP Financial Marketing Pocket Book 1997*

2) *Pensions Pocket Book 1997 in conjunction with Bacon & Woodrow.*

3) *Moneyfacts*

Lincoln is a marketing group regulated by the Personal Investment Authority providing life assurance, pensions and unit trusts.

CITY CAREERS

TRAINEESHIPS AND MANAGEMENT DEVELOPMENT PROGRAMMES 1998

THE CHALLENGE – Men still dominate most financial services companies. Times are changing and the senior female managers in City Financial Partners, part of the Lincoln Group, are successfully redressing the balance. Would you like to join them?

THE POSITION – City Financial Partners is a true meritocracy with progress from trainee to early management and beyond being based on assessed performance. After training and professional exams, you will be involved in the development of private clients. You will deal right across the markets from introducing people to private banking, to healthcare, pensions and investments.

TRAINING – A highly structured and comprehensive training programme is mandatory commencing on appointment. The training covers every aspect of the financial services industry and detailed exposition of the products developed to serve the varied needs of the marketplace. The form of the training programme ranges from disciplined studies with professional examinations to a carefully structured long term "on the job" programme which bring out individual skills and demonstrates their practical application.

APPLICANT PROFILE – Applications are invited from individuals now aged over 23 interested in a career that has no artificial limitations. Although the majority of our intake come from degree backgrounds, character, personality and a desire to achieve are the real indicators of career potential. Some of our most successful partners are not graduates.

REWARDS – The rewards are high both financially and in terms of personal growth. On achieving partnership status it is possible to move into management and lead your own teams or specialise in a particular market or industry sector.

HOW TO APPLY – For further information and an opportunity to view the company first-hand, call Elizabeth Hill or Emma Smith on 0171 379 5995 x 7803, or send your CV with a covering note to:
Emma Smith, City Financial Partners,
Centre Point, New Oxford Street, London WC1A 1DD.

2
Choosing the best savings account

Banks and building societies offer a wide range of savings accounts. When choosing an account, there are several questions to consider:

- What is the minimum investment?
- What are the rules on paying in more money?
- How easily can you get at your savings?
- How often is the interest paid?
- Is the interest fixed or variable?
- How much interest can you earn? Generally speaking, the longer you can tie your money up for, and the larger the amount you have to invest, the higher the interest rate.

    Many accounts have tiered rates, so the more money you invest, the better the return.
- Are you getting the best rate? Check the savings rate tables published in the money pages of national newspapers including Wednesday's *Express*. Consider postal accounts, offered by several building societies. Because these accounts are cheap to run, they often pay better rates. The 'savings bible' is MoneyFacts — phone 01603 476100 for details.

Tax on savings

Bank and building society income is taxed. If you pay no more than basic or lower 20 per cent tax rate you need do nothing more. Higher rate taxpayers will have extra to pay. This may be settled through a twice yearly bill resulting from self-assess-

As you'd expect, we offer you a plum rate on our instant access savings account.

Pick a high interest Instant Access Savings Account at Sainsbury's Bank and you will earn interest on balances from as little as £1. Naturally, we also offer 24 hour telephone banking and you can withdraw your money free of charge from over 14,000 cash dispensers within the Link network.

Enjoy the fruits of fresher thinking in banking. For more details call free anytime quoting ref S9023.

SAINSBURY'S BANK

FRESH BANKING™ FROM SAINSBURY'S

FREEPHONE 0500 40 50 60

ment tax returns. Non-taxpayers can reclaim the tax or even better, register to receive it gross (using form R85).

Tax Exempt Special Savings Accounts

TESSAs are tax-free accounts run by banks and building societies, designed to run for five years. You can save up to £3000 in the first year and up to £1800 in each of the next four years, provided you don't put in more than £9000 in total.

But even if you think you may want access to your savings before five years are up, a TESSA can still be a good bet, since they often pay good rates, and the most you stand to lose is the tax relief. There may be specific penalties on top if you have opted for a fixed rate TESSA and wish to cash in before the five years are up.

Minimum investments vary but many will accept regular monthly savings from £1 upwards. The maximum monthly saving allowed by the Inland Revenue is £150.

You are free to transfer your TESSA from one bank or building society to another, but there may be penalties. And some TESSA providers pay a bonus to savers who stay loyal for the full five years.

When your TESSA matures, you can transfer the capital up to £9000 into a new TESSA but you cannot add to it or leave the interest. New TESSAs stop in April 1999 when they will be replaced by Individual Savings Accounts. Existing TESSAs will continue their lives. When they mature, the capital — but not accumulated interest — can be placed in the ISA, irrespective of other investments.

Tax: Tax-free.
Suitable for: Medium term savers. Especially good for well-paid women who can save higher rate tax on their investment, but a sensible option for anyone who wants to save tax-free.

National Savings

National Savings offers a range of accounts, including:

- *Granny Bonds:* Granny Bonds (officially called Pensioners Guaranteed Income Bond) are open to the over 65s. They pay a fixed rate which is set from time to time. At the time of writing it was 6.10 per cent gross over five years. The minimum investment is £500 and the maximum is £50,000. Interest is paid into your bank or building society account each month. Capital withdrawals are subject to a 60-day no interest notice or, if you want the money urgently, a 90-day loss of interest.
  Tax: Interest is paid with no tax taken off but you are liable for tax at your highest rate.
  Suitable for: Pensioners who want a fixed return and can tie up their money for five years. But the 65 lower age limit is a big drawback for many women who retired at 60.
- *First Option Bonds:* These are aimed at basic rate taxpayers. You can invest a minimum of £1000 up to a maximum of £250,000. The interest rate is 6.50 per cent net of basic rate tax on sums up to £20,000 and 6.75 per cent on larger amounts, fixed for one year. At the end of 12 months you can either cash in, or opt to reinvest at a new fixed one-year rate. If you withdraw in the first year, you get no interest. After that if you cash in part-way through a year, you will only get half the normal rate for that year, so it's best to cash in on the bond's anniversary.
  Tax: Interest is paid with basic rate tax taken off automatically. Non-taxpayers and lower rate taxpayers can reclaim tax, higher rate taxpayers have to pay more.
- *NS Certificates:* The current 46th issue pays a guaranteed five-year return of 4.8 per cent. Minimum investment is £100, maximum is £10,000, but you can reinvest all previously matured certificates without limit. Returns are reduced if you cash in early, and there is no interest at all if you cash in during the first year.
  Tax: Tax-free.
- *Suitable for:* Medium-term lump sum savers, well-paid women who want to save higher rate tax.

- *Index-linked Certificates:* Similar to ordinary certificates, except that the current 13th Issue pays a return of 2.25 per cent on top of inflation, guaranteed for five years.
  Tax: Tax-free.
  Suitable for: Medium-term lump sum savers worried about inflation, well-paid women who are higher rate taxpayers.
- *Capital Bonds:* The minimum investment is £100 and the maximum is £250,000. The current rate is 6.00 per cent gross, fixed for five years, though the rate is reduced if you cash in early.
  Tax: Taxable. An unattractive feature is taxpayers must pay tax on the interest each year, even though they won't receive it for five years.
  Suitable for: Medium-term lump sum savers; non-taxpayers; a good investment for children.
- *Children's Bonus Bonds:* These are an ideal investment if you want to put some money away for children or grand-children, because they pay a high tax-free rate of interest. They can be bought by anyone aged 16 or over for a child under 16. Once purchased, they can be held until the youngster is 21.

  Minimum investment is £25, maximum £1000. The interest rate is 6.00 per cent, guaranteed for five years.
  Tax: Tax-free.
  Suitable for: Mums, grandmothers, aunts, godmothers or anyone else who wants to invest for kids.

All interest rates are liable to change for new investors at short notice. But savers already in fixed-rate products will not experience any change.

3
Making the stock market work for you

The stock market has a reputation as a casino where only the professional gamblers stand a chance of winning. But investing in stocks and shares is well within the reach of the woman — or man — in the street. In fact, you are probably a stock market investor already without even knowing it. If you have a pension or an endowment policy, your money is indirectly going into stocks and shares.

Provided you spread your risks and invest for the long term, putting money into the stock market can be both profitable and enjoyable.

Stocks and shares

Many women have already dabbled in the stock market by buying shares in privatisation issues such as BT or British Gas. Shares can be risky — both BT and British Gas have had bright and boring times — but if you are astute enough to pick the right companies, you can make good profits.

- Experts recommend you do not invest directly in shares unless you have at least £20,000 at your disposal to channel into 5–10 different companies. That is around the minimum sum that will give you a decent spread of risk — if you put too much into one single share, you are very vulnerable if the price falls.
- It is not worth investing small amounts in shares because stockbroker's commission can wipe out all your profits. Smaller investors are normally better off sticking to unit or investment trusts.

Government privatisations are really the only exception, because there are no buying charges and the price is usually pitched so investors stand to make a profit. The only problem is there is now little left to privatise and the initial prices are now realistic rather than giveaway.

- If you do have the wherewithal to build up a share portfolio, or if you inherited one from someone else, your first decision is whether to manage it yourself or to hand it over to a professional manager.

- Running your own portfolio profitably is hard work — though some women have done so highly successfully. You will have to spend a great deal of time learning about investments by reading background material and scouring the financial press. Most investors of this type use a low-cost stockbroker service, which is designed simply to carry out your buy and sell instructions without giving you any advice. This is known as 'execution only'.

INVESTORLINK
LOW COST SHARE DEALING

When it comes to picking up bargains, most men would concede that women have no equal. That is why our readers will warm to a share dealing service that costs as little as £5 per transaction. Called Investorlink, it was the first service to introduce this economical approach to playing the market.

A phone call puts you in touch with any one of Investorlink's more than helpful staff who confirm and action your instructions smoothly and efficiently. For deals up to £500, your first instruction will cost £15, the second instruction £10, and a mere £5 thereafter. Maximum discount is limited to eight orders in one day. A similar formula applies from £501 to £1,700, reducing to £7. From £1,701 to £5,000 the rate is 1% with a maximum of £50 for deals up to £20,000. Higher aunts by negotiation. Also available, family deals for selling.

Investorlink is a division of Walker Crips Weddle Beck Plc. which was established in 1914 and is fully listed on The London Stock Exchange.

For an application form,
call freephone 0800 289 600

- You can opt for a stockbroking service with advice, which will be more expensive. With this option, you will still be responsible for making the ultimate dealing decisions, and for valuing the portfolio each year and handling the income and capital gains tax due.
- If you have a large portfolio, you can choose a portfolio management service where everything is done for you. Some managers insist on making all the investment decisions themselves — others allow you the final say.
- Or you can pick with a pin. Academic studies show this method, officially known as 'the Random Walk' works just as well as the professionals if you can invest in a good spread of different shares for the long term.
- Share dividends come with tax at 20 per cent deducted at source. Basic and lower rate taxpayers don't have to pay any more, but higher rate taxpayers must top up their payment to 40 per cent. Non-taxpayers can reclaim the tax. Capital gains tax at your highest tax rate is payable on profits. But you have an annual exemption of £6800 in the 1998/9 tax year.

Unit and investment trusts

Unit and investment trusts are most suitable for long-term investors who are prepared to take the risk of losing some of their money in return for greater potential rewards than the building society. Your money is pooled with that of other investors in the trust, and invested in a wide range of shares and other assets, so it spreads your risk. So far, no unit trust has gone bust — although one or two have 'disappeared' through fraud or incompetence.

- You can cash in without penalty whenever you choose. But it is best not to put money you may need in a hurry into the stock market — you may lose out if you are forced to sell at a point when prices are low.
- Most unit trusts and investment trust savings schemes set

minimum lump sum investments of £250–1000 or £25–50 per month. Invesment trust savings schemes can be particularly good value in terms of charges — most make a minimal charge of 0.2 per cent. With unit trusts, there is normally a 5–6 per cent initial charge, and you will normally have to pay annual management charges of 1–1.5 per cent.

Investment trusts can produce higher rewards but their structure can magnify losses when share prices fall. Open Ended Investment Companies are a new style fund type which is gradually replacing unit trusts. They are more easily understood.

Personal Equity Plans

Personal Equity Plans stop in April 1999 but until then up to £6000 of UK or European Union shares can be tax-sheltered in a PEP each tax year. The £6000 limit also applies to unit and investment trusts provided at least half of the trust's assets are in the UK or the European Union.

Company bonds, convertibles and preference shares are also eligible for the full £6000 PEP allowance. These sound complicated, but are basically investments paying a fixed income, and are generally somewhat less risky than shares. However, they are not totally safe building society-type investments either, so ask your PEP seller for a full explanation of the risks. Many unit and investment trust PEPs allow regular contributions from £30–50 per month.

- Unit and investment trusts are tax-free in a PEP, otherwise income is paid net of lower rate tax. Non-taxpayers and lower rate taxpayers can reclaim the tax, higher rate taxpayers must pay extra. Profits, after an 'inflation' allowance, are liable to capital gains tax, though there is an annual exemption of £6500 in the 1997/8 tax year.
- These investments are risky, but offer the chance of higher rewards than the building society. They are suitable for long-term savers who are prepared to take a risk and well-paid women who want to save higher rate tax.

Individual Savings Accounts

These will replace both PEPs and TESSAs from April 1999, although you will be allowed to continue with any money you have invested in either. ISA holders can save £5,000 a year without any tax liabilities — £7,000 in 1999–2000. Stock market investments, including unit and investment trusts, will not have a geographic limit. Up to £1,000 a year — £3000 in 1999–2000 — can be as a cash deposit. And a further £1,000 within the limit can be invested in life-insurance funds.

Endowment policies

Endowment policies are a long-term option for regular savers, with annual returns in the region of 8–10 per cent. You commit yourself to saving a set regular sum each month for a given period; usually ten or 25 years.

- With-profits endowments are a relatively safe way of gaining exposure to stock market growth potential. Life company funds invest in a mixture of shares, property and fixed interest investments, and your return comes in the form of regular bonuses, which, once added, cannot be removed. There is also a terminal bonus when the policy matures. This can be a major slice of your profit.
- Proceeds from an endowment are tax-free, though the fund in which your premiums are invested is taxable. The biggest problem with these policies is that if you want to cash in before the end of the term — as a large proportion of policy holders do — you will get a very low surrender value. In the first five years, it could be less than you have put in. In the first two years, it could be nothing. Only sign up for an endowment if you are sure you can last the course.
- Endowments are a relatively safe way of investing in the stock market. But because much of the return comes in the form of the maturity bonus, your total return is uncertain right until the end.

Friendly society plans

Friendly society plans are tax-free, and operate in a similar way to an endowment policy, with similar returns. They are boosted by tax freedom, but most feature high costs which can erode the taxation benefit. The most you can invest is £25 per month or £270 a year into a plan, designed to last ten years. Beware of cashing in early, though, since the returns can be heavily reduced.

Friendly society plans are a very tax-efficient way mothers, grandmothers and aunts can invest for a child. Many friendly societies offer 'half-plans' for those who want to save for more than one child but cannot afford £25 per month each.

They are suitable for long-term small savers, mums, grand-mothers, aunts and godmothers or anyone else who wants to invest for children.

The recent changes by several major building societies which have converted into banks and listed on the London Stock Exchange have created a new generation of shareholders - several million, many of whom are women.

Becoming a shareholder for the first time provides an ideal opportunity to review your financial situation and to consider whether you might like to build up a portfolio, or collection, of shares using the windfall shares from your building society as the starting point. Shareholding, and its implications for you, are nowhere near as complex as many people believe and there are plenty of sources of information available should you be starting more or less from scratch.

With political parties of all complexions emphasising that the welfare state can no longer provide for everyone in the longer term, it is more than ever important for each of us to make provision for the future. Despite the ups and downs of the stock market, particularly at times of uncertainty in world markets, research shows that in any ten year period an investment in shares out-performs savings made through other methods, such as building societies and deposit accounts.

Your shareholding can help your financial provision for the future in two different ways: by providing income in the forms of dividends, which are paid usually twice a year; and by helping your capital to grow. You will share in the rewards if the company does well, although you will need to be aware that a poor performance by the company, as well as general economic factors, can make the price of shares go down.

This is one of the reasons why it is sensible to build up a portfolio of shares in different companies. This will provide you with some protection so that if one of your companies is experiencing a lean time, you may continue to have income and capital growth from the others.

Stockbrokers are able to deal with the needs of the millions of new shareholders, providing advice if you require it; or simply buying and selling on your behalf. The price you pay for this will naturally depend on the level of service you require from your stockbroker.

The London Stock Exchange has produced a guide - Share Ownership for All - which is available free of charge from the Public Information department (see advertisement opposite). This provides information about shareholding in straightforward language and explains how to choose a stockbroker. Access to the stock market has never been easier than it is today: there are over 120 firms of stockbrokers, many with offices across the UK, in addition to the high street banks, all of whom offer share dealing services.

Whether you prefer to receive advice from a stockbroker, or manage your money on your own, there is a service to meet your needs. And to support you further, there is an extensive range of information available nowadays on all aspects of stockmarket investment whether you prefer to consult a stockbroker, plough through the media, surf the net or browse in a bookshop. But which ever route you choose, there is no time like the present to look carefully at your financial situation, to assess your needs for the future and to start making provision for the years ahead.

If you'd like the basic facts about stock market investment, we'd like to share them with you.

Whether you have received windfall shares or would simply like to find out what the stock market can do for you, call **0171 797 1372** for our free booklet, "Share Ownership for All" or visit our website at www.londonstockex.co.uk

GET YOUR SHARE OF GREAT BRITISH COMPANIES

Get Share Aware
0171 797 1372
Free Information Pack

London **STOCK EXCHANGE**

Gilts

Gilts are basically IOUs from the government. They pay a fixed rate of return, or coupon, usually every six months and the government guarantees to repay a fixed capital value, normally £100, when they mature. For instance, Treasury 10 per cent 2003 means the coupon is 10 per cent and the government will give you back £100 in 2003.

- Gilts can be bought and sold on the stock market. You are unlikely to pay exactly £100, so the actual percentage return you receive won't usually be the same as the coupon.
- If you keep a gilt until it matures, you know exactly what return you will get. If you sell before maturity, you could make a gain — or a loss. Bear in mind that if you pay more than £100 for your gilts and keep them to maturity, you are locking into a capital loss. These make little sense for tax-paying women — leave them to the professionals.
- You can buy gilts easily and cheaply through the National Savings Stock Register in major post offices. The minimum commission for purchases and for sales is generally cheaper than a stockbroker. You can also invest in index-linked gilts, which offer some protection against inflation. Interest on gilts bought through the Post Office is paid gross but is taxable, but you will not receive any advice as to the suitability or otherwise of your decision. Capital gains are tax-free.
  There is no risk to your capital unless you sell before the gilts mature.
- Gilts are suitable for investors who want a fixed income and guaranteed capital return.

More information

You can get more information about unit trusts from:

The Association of Unit Trusts and Investment Funds
65 Kingsway
London WC2B 6TD
Tel: 0181-207 1361 (8am to 11pm daily)

More detail on investment trusts is available from:

The Association of Investment Trust Companies
Durrant House
8–13 Chiswell Street
London EC1Y 4YY
Tel: 0171-588 5347

You can obtain a list of private client stockbrokers from:

The Association of Private Client Investment Managers and
    Stockbrokers
112 Middlesex Street
London E1 7HY
(Postal enquiries only)

The wider share ownership organisation ProShare offers a range of information services to private sharebuyers:

ProShare
Library Chambers
13–14 Basinghall Street
London EC2V 5BQ
Tel: 0171-600 0984

4
Tax matters

Tax is an inescapable part of your finances. The tax rules affect your pay, your savings income, your mortgage and any profits you make on investments. All women, whether married, single, separated or divorced, are responsible for their own tax affairs in the eyes of the Inland Revenue. In the chapters on savings and investments, tax-free investments have been pointed out. But here, we look at the workings of the tax system, and how you might make some tax savings.

Your tax-free allowances

The tax year runs from April to April. Each tax year you are given a tax allowance. This is the amount of income you can receive before you start to pay tax. Everyone has a 'Personal Allowance', and you may have other allowances, such as a Married Couple's Allowance or Additional Personal Allowance. If your income is less than your allowances, you are a non-taxpayer.

For 1998/9, the allowances are:

Personal Allowance:	£4195
Married Couple's Allowance	£1900

- The Married Couple's Allowance is automatically given to your husband. But you can elect to share it equally between you by informing the authorities you wish to do so before the end of the previous tax year — you don't need your husband's permission to do this. If you both agree, you can have the full Married Couple's Allowance yourself.
- Tax relief on the Married Couple's Allowance is 15 per cent in cash terms, whatever tax rate you pay, so the MCA is worth £285, provided you have sufficient income to cover it.

In April 1999, the rate will fall to 10 per cent, so the relief will be worth £190 a year in cash terms.

- If you are single, separated, widowed or divorced and have a child or children living with you, you are entitled to an Additional Personal Allowance of £1900. Relief is given in the same way as the Married Couples' Allowance. Your child must be under 16, or in full-time education at university, college or school.
- There are special tax reliefs for widows of any age. In the tax year your husband dies, you receive the Married Couple's Allowance. You can also claim the Widow's Bereavement Allowance — the same sum as the Married Couple's Allowance — in the year after his death.

Allowances for older women and couples

- Over 65s are entitled to higher personal allowances. In 1998/9 these are:

Personal allowance age	65–74	£5410
	over 75	£5600
Married Couple's Allowance	65–74	£3305
	over 75	£3345

- For single women and widows, your higher Personal Allowance is reduced by £1 for each £2 of income you receive above £16,200 in the 1998/9 tax year. But your allowance will not be allowed to fall below the basic Personal Allowance. Husband and wife each have their own £16,200 income limit.
- Higher Married Couple's Allowances are granted on the basis of the age of the older spouse in the tax year. The value of these is limited to 15 per cent and will fall to 10 per cent in April 1999. Spouses each have their own £16,200 income limit.

Income tax rates and bands

The first £4300 of any income after your personal and other allowances is taxed at 20 per cent; that between £4301 and

£27,100 in the 1998/9 tax year is taxed at the basic rate of 23 per cent. Taxable income of more than £27,100 is taxed at 40 per cent in 1998/9.

Tax and your job

- If you work for an employer, you will usually be taxed through the Pay As You Earn or PAYE system. Your employer deducts the tax you have to pay out of your wages or salary before you receive them.
- Each tax year, the Inland Revenue issues you with a PAYE code, telling your employer how much of your pay is free of tax. The last number is missed off. So, for instance, if your PAYE code is 352L, it tells your employer you receive the personal allowance, and should get £3525 of tax-free pay. This figure takes personal allowances and pensions on the plus side and subtracts tax on company perks such as cars and medical insurance.

Income tax on your savings and investments

- Interest on bank or building society savings accounts is paid net of basic rate tax, but it is taxable at your highest rate. If you are a 20 or 23 per cent taxpayer, your liability is fully covered. Higher rate taxpayers must pay an extra 20 per cent.
- Dividends from shares, unit trusts and investment trusts are paid with tax of 20 per cent already deducted. If you are a non-taxpayer, you can claim the tax back. If you are a lower or basic rate taxpayer, you have no further tax to pay, but if you are a higher rate taxpayer, you must pay a further 20 per cent tax. Non-taxpayers will no longer be able to reclaim tax on shares and share based investments from April 1999. But they will continue to receive a tax rebate on bonds and government stocks if they apply.
- If you and your husband have joint savings or investments, the tax authorities assume you receive half the income each no matter whose money paid for them.

Capital gains tax

If you make a profit when you sell certain assets, such as shares or a valuable painting, you may be liable for capital gains tax. Capital gains tax may be payable when you dispose of an asset, whether you sell it or give it away, so you can't avoid the tax by making presents of your assets.

Fortunately, many of your main assets are exempt from capital gains tax, including:

- your only or main home;
- gifts between husband and wife;
- private motor cars;
- bank and building society savings and National Savings accounts;
- betting winnings and National Lottery gains;
- gilts (government stocks);
- there are also complicated reliefs if you sell a business.

You also have an annual gains tax exemption — £6800 in the 1998/9 tax year. Husband and wife each have their own exemption.

Any profits above the exemption from shares, unit trusts or investment trusts are added to your taxable income and taxed at your highest rate. A substantial gain can easily catapult you into the highest 40 per cent tax band. Up to April 1998, you could reduce your gains by the rate of inflation. Thereafter, a tax 'taper' was introduced which reduces the rate for assets held for periods from three years up to ten years, where the taper will stop.

Inheritance tax

Many people underestimate their assets and wrongly assume that inheritance tax, charged at 40 per cent if the value of your estate exceeds £223,000 (the nil rate band in the 1998/9 tax year) does not affect them. So if your estate, including the family home, is worth £273,000, your potential inheritance tax bill is £50,000 × 40% = £20,000.

Married couples each have their own £223,000 nil rate band.

Anything to declare?

If you receive a tax return, you *must* fill it in fully and honestly, and return it promptly, otherwise you may be charged interest and penalties.

Women who are basic rate taxpayers and are taxed under PAYE will often not be sent a tax return.

But if you have other income, for instance from a second job or from letting out a property, it is your responsibility to notify the tax authorities, whether or not they send you a return.

Tax saving tips

- If you are a non-taxpayer ask for form R85 at your bank or building society so you can register to receive interest on your savings with no tax deducted.
- Married couples should consider transferring income-producing assets into the name of the partner paying the lowest rate of tax. For instance, if you are a 40 per cent taxpayer and your husband is paying a lower rate, transferring some of your savings into his name could save 20 per cent tax. But the assets you transfer become his — you cannot attach strings to the transfer.
- Always check your tax code — the Revenue can make mistakes leaving you paying too much tax.
- Make the most of tax-free savings and investment opportunities. These include:
  - National Savings certificates and index-linked certificates;
  - Personal Equity Plans and TESSAs (to be replaced by Individual Savings Accounts).

  More details of these are given in the chapters on savings and investments.
- You can reduce potential inheritance tax bills by making a tax-efficient will. Gifts made within your lifetime can also reduce the bill. Most gifts are Potentially Exempt Transfers

— there is no tax to pay provided you live for seven years after making the gift but the gift must be made 'without reservation'. You cannot ask for it back if you need it, nor can you 'borrow' it; so make sure you can afford it. There are a number of inheritance tax avoidance plans; many are untried and could fail to save your family the tax; also, most are expensive to operate.

Some gifts are totally tax-free, including:

– a gift of up to £3000 to any one person;
– gifts from parents of up to £5000 to a child on their marriage, and up to £2500 from grandparents;
– an unlimited number of small gifts of up to £250 each year.

Your local tax enquiry office should be able to help with questions — the number is listed in the telephone directory.

5
Women at work

In the bad old days women had to choose between a career and a family. Now, whether through choice or economic necessity, most women have to juggle both. Changes in society mean women are more likely to be involved in paid employment than ever before. Many companies are cutting back on traditional male full-time posts and replacing them with part-time positions likely to be filled by women. In many households, women are becoming the main or only breadwinners.

By the start of the 1990s, women in the UK had the second highest rate of participation in the labour force of any European country, and the highest number of women in employment. Now, around 65 per cent of women work outside the home, and women account for one in four of the self-employed, according to government statistics.

It means the majority of women will need to tackle a range of financial issues connected with paid employment, including maternity benefits, your rights when it comes to equal pay for equal work, and combining a career with a family.

Equal pay for equal work

It would be very rare to find a man being paid more than a woman for doing exactly the same job nowadays. Equal Pay regulations brought in in 1984 state that a woman can claim 'equal pay for work of equal value' to a man working for the same employer. The Sex Discrimination Act of 1975 (along with subsequent amendments in 1986 and 1989) makes it unlawful for employers to discriminate against anyone on the grounds of their sex. The Act covers recruitment, training, promotion, dismissal and retirement.

But the great male/female pay divide still persists. Average full-time female earnings are currently just 80 per cent of the average male wage, according to the government. Even at the top, figures show female executives earn around £60,000 a year, a quarter less than the average male executive in similar work.

There is no easy answer on how individual women can make sure their work is not undervalued. Training and working for relevant professional qualifications should help boost your salary and open more options on the job market. Contact your local Careers Service, or speak to your manager or company training department.

If you are a victim of sex discrimination at work, you can take your case to an Industrial Tribunal. Go to your local Employment Service office and ask for application form IT1 or IT(Scot) in Scotland.

Sexual harassment is now recognised as a factor that can hold back women at work, stopping them from doing their job and lowering morale. The Equal Opportunities Commission has launched new guidelines for dealing with it.

The European Commission Code of Conduct defines sexual harassment as: 'Unwanted conduct of a sexual nature based on sex affecting the dignity of men and women at work. This can include unwelcome physical, verbal or non verbal conduct.'

In other words, it can include lewd remarks or glances, requests for sexual favours and physical contact.

Under the Sex Discrimination Act, the employer is liable for discriminatory acts by employees whilst at work. There is no limit to the sums that can be awarded in cases taken to industrial tribunals. But tribunals are still held in public with no restrictions on newspapers reporting even the most salacious details or taking your photograph. This can be intimidating.

Equal opportunities

Women still have a long way to go to achieve the same career status as men. According to government statistics, out of

144,000 managers of large companies, only 8 per cent are female. The ratio of men to women holding public appointments is 3 : 1. In professions such as medicine, the law and education the picture is no better. Fewer than 15 per cent of medical consultants are women, even though half of all medical students are female. Only 3 per cent of professors and principal lecturers at universities are female, and women account for just 5 per cent of circuit judges.

But fortunately, that's beginning to change. Some employers are streets ahead of others when it comes to the treatment of female staff — it's worth researching if you are job hunting. Companies that have signed the Opportunity 2000 initiative launched in October 1991 have committed themselves to the aim of 'increasing the quality and quantity of women's participation in the workforce'. They include Abbey National, Boots the Chemist, Sainsburys, several universities, BT and WH Smith.

Opportunity 2000 now has 275 members, accounting for more than a quarter of the UK workforce. It claims significant successes since launch. Amongst its members, women hold 25 per cent of managerial posts, more than double the percentage in UK top companies as a whole. At director level, women account for 8 per cent of posts amongst Opportunity 2000 members, compared with less than 3 per cent elsewhere.

When taken seriously, policies to advance women can be highly successful. For instance, Barclays Bank, an Opportunity 2000 member, has doubled the number of female managers in a decade by bringing in a range of woman-friendly working practices, including career break schemes for women and men after the birth of a baby, emergency carer's leave, job-sharing and term-time only contracts. These are, however, still a comparative rarity among the female workforce as a whole.

More information

The Equal Opportunities Commission aims to eliminate sex discrimination at work. It publishes a leaflet, *Sexual Harassment: What You Can Do About It*, available from:

EOC
Overseas House
Quay Street
Manchester M3 3HN
Tel: 0161-833 9244
Price £1.

6
Buying your own home

Your home is likely to be your biggest financial asset as well as a place to live. So you are not only trying to find a dream dwelling — or as near to it as possible — but also aiming to ensure value for money.

Because of the trend towards later marriages and greater female earning power, more single women are buying a home on their own than ever before, rather than waiting until they marry or move in with a partner.

But whether you are buying a home as a single person or with a partner, friend, or relative, it pays to be clued up on the costs and on your responsibilities as a mortgage holder.

Your first step towards finding a new home is to work out how much you can afford and how you intend to repay it.

Picking the best mortgage

Single women can usually borrow up to three times their salary and couples can take a loan of up to two and a half times joint incomes, or three times the higher income and one times the lower salary — sometimes higher multiples are allowed. Try to leave yourself some money in hand each month in case interest rates rise. Nowadays it is unusual for borrowers to be granted a 100 per cent mortgage — you will normally have to find a deposit of at least 5 per cent.

Any high street bank or building society will advise you on mortgages. The two best known types of loan are repayment and interest-only (usually based on endowment policies) mortgages. You also have to consider whether you want to take out a fixed rate mortgage or one where the interest rate varies.

Repayment mortgages are the simplest type. Your monthly payments are used to reduce the capital as well as the interest. At first, the capital goes down slowly, but at the end of the term, usually 25 years, you will have repaid the loan in full.

With an endowment mortgage, you pay interest only throughout the life of the loan, and you also pay premiums to an endowment policy, which you hope will give you enough to repay the loan at the end of its term, and perhaps leave you with a tax-free lump sum as well. But endowments only work if you last the full course. They can be bad value if you decide to leave home owning — you rent, move abroad or get a home with your job — or if your relationship breaks down and you need to share assets with a partner.

These are the most popular types of home loan. But remember you will pay high commission and costs on the endowment policy. Never cash in an endowment when you move — the return will be very poor. You can always take out another policy to top up if you need to cover a larger mortgage.

Homebuyers can also take out a pension or a PEP mortgage. Pension mortgages are similar to endowment-linked loans, except it is your pension that is used as backing. They are very tax-efficient for higher rate taxpayers, because you receive tax relief at your highest rate on contributions to the pension. But you have to pay off the home loan out of your pension lump sum, which will reduce your income when you retire.

With a PEP mortgage, you make monthly payments into a tax-free Personal Equity Plan, which invests in unit or investment trusts or shares, and pay interest only off your mortgage. Again, you hope your PEP will produce enough to pay off the loan at the end of the term.

PEPs are more flexible than endowments because you can cash in at any time without penalty. It means if your plan performs well, you can pay off your mortgage early, and save yourself a chunk of interest. But they are also more risky, because they are linked to the stock market. However you can always switch to a less volatile investment near the end of the loan as a safety first move. PEPs will be replaced by Individual Savings Accounts in April 1999. The level of tax rebate will be cut on that date, but homebuyers will be able to use the ISA in much the same way as they use PEPs.

Tables showing the best mortgage rates are printed in the personal finance sections of newspapers. The *Express* publishes rates every Wednesday.

Be careful when taking out a tempting discount offer, though. There is often a catch. The discount may run for a short period only, there may be heavy penalties if you have to move mortgages within a given time, often five years, and you may have to take out expensive insurance policies through the lender to qualify for the cheap rate.

The tax relief on mortgage interest, known as MIRAS or Mortgage Interest Relief at Source, has been progressively cut. It is 10 per cent on the interest on the first £30,000 of your home loan. At 8 per cent, that is worth £240 a year in cash terms on an interest only loan.

Variable or fixed rate?

Fixed rate mortgages, as their name suggests, set your repayments at a guaranteed rate for a given period, normally from one to five years. With a variable rate loan, your instalments go up and down according to interest rate movements.

One advantage of a fixed loan is that you know exactly how much you will be paying over the term, and you will not suffer if interest rates go up. But you could lose out if you fix your repayments and then interest rates go down. You will also have to pay an arrangement fee of £200–£300, and there are heavy penalties if you want to change mortgage before the fixed term has ended. Some mortgages are 'capped' — you know you cannot pay more than the standard rate but your interest bill can fall if bank rates are cut.

Buying costs

There are a whole host of hidden extras. Fees on a £50,000 home with a 95 per cent mortgage add up to around £1500. Make sure you budget for:

- A deposit of at least 5 per cent of the property value
- Loan arrangement fees of £200–300 on fixed-rate mortgages.
- A report on the condition of the property and valuation, costing around £260 on a £50,000 home. If the property is old or unusual, get a full structural survey.
- Find a qualified solicitor to handle the conveyancing and paperwork. Legal fees vary depending on your area and the solicitor you use. Expect to spend £400–£500 on a £50,000 property.
- Local search at £50 and £100 land registry fee.
- Mortgage indemnity premiums for those borrowing more than three quarters of the property value — about £700 on a £50,000 purchase. These can go up very steeply as you pass 'thresholds' such as 75, 80, 85 and 90 per cent, although many major lenders now only impose the charge if you are borrowing more than 90 per cent of the property's value.
- Stamp duty of 1 per cent on homes bought for more than £60,000 and below £250,000. This is levied on the entire amount — not just the balance over £60,000. Homebuyers with properties between £250,001 and £500,000 pay 2 per cent and the levy on larger amounts is 3 per cent — all payable on the full purchase price and not the amount over the rate change threshold.
- Buyers will also need to set aside some money for removal expenses, redecoration and new furniture. Check the removal firm has adequate insurance in case of breakages.
- Don't forget monthly outgoings such as council tax, gas and electricity bills and water rates. Ask the present owners about average bills and costs.

- You will have to pay for compulsory house buildings insurance premiums each month as well as your mortgage instalments. Home contents cover is not obligatory but recommended, although buying buildings and contents cover from the lender may be obligatory if you take out a discount or cashback loan. These policies are usually pricey. It may also be sensible to take out an insurance policy to cover your monthly payments if you have an accident, fall ill or lose your job. New borrowers will not receive any Social Security help for the first nine months, and the mortgage ceiling has been cut to £100,000. So it's more important than ever to take out your own insurance. But redundancy and sickness policies are expensive. Avoid them if you feel you or your partner could continue to pay the loan.

Finding your new home

- Be specific on the size and type of property you are looking for, which areas you would prefer, and your price range.
- Don't waste time viewing properties you know will not be suitable — but be prepared to be flexible. You are unlikely to find complete perfection.
- When you find a property you want to buy, make an offer through the estate agent.
- Estate agents act for the seller, not the buyer. That means it is the agent's main job to persuade you to buy at the highest possible price. Don't be afraid to bargain — sellers usually set their asking price higher than they actually expect to receive.
- It is a criminal offence for estate agents to make false or misleading statements about a property offered for sale. But they will still try to put on the best possible gloss.
- Don't be influenced by superficial factors such as decoration or attractive fittings — they don't add much value and you are likely to want to redecorate anyway.
- Consider whether your new home is convenient for shops, good schools, public transport, parks, recreational facilities and so on.

- Be clear about exactly what the selling price includes. For instance, will the seller be leaving behind fixtures such as fireplaces, and fittings such as carpets and shelves?
- Is the property freehold or leasehold? Many flats are lease-hold. Be wary of buying anything with a short lease — seventy years is a good rule of thumb. Don't go below it unless the property is unusual, very desirable or very cheap.

Moving in

Once your survey has been done, your mortgage agreed and your solicitor has completed various searches, you should be ready to exchange contracts. At this stage, you pay over your deposit and you are committed to buy.

The home actually changes ownership some time after exchange, normally about 28 days.

Your solicitor arranges for the mortgage money to be paid to the seller's solicitor and you can then collect the keys. This is known as completion. The system is different in Scotland.

When you move, you will need to contact the gas, water, electricity and telephone companies to transfer the accounts into your name. You will also need to inform friends, your employer, your doctor and dentist that you have moved. If you have savings or investments, remember to notify the provider of your new address, along with the DVLA if you drive a car.

Joint mortgages

Couples buying a home together should sit down and agree the proportion of the home loan and bills each will pay. It is also worth considering how you want to deal with the investment plans you are using to back the mortgage. For instance, taking out a joint endowment can cause problems if you split up, as the policy may have to be cashed in, often incurring big penalties. But there is no reason why each partner cannot take out their own policy or PEP to back their slice of the mortgage, and simply carry on with it in the event of a break-up. You may have to make special life insurance arrangements to ensure the debt is paid off in full if one partner dies, however.

You also need to consider the question of ownership of the home. Most married couples are 'joint tenants', which means they both own the whole property jointly. If one or other dies, the whole property automatically passes to the survivor, whatever is written in the will.

The other form of ownership is to be 'tenants in common.' Here, the interests of each partner are fixed, usually 50:50, but couples can agree on a different proportion. If one partner dies, their share goes into their estate and can be left to whoever they please.

Women buying a home with a husband or partner should be aware that when they take out a joint mortgage, both parties are potentially liable for the full debt. So if your husband or partner cannot or will not pay, the lender may well chase you for the money. Your ownership arrangements are irrelevant — even if you only own 30 per cent of your home as a tenant in common, you are responsible for the full mortgage instalments.

Coping with mortgage problems

If you run into difficulty with your repayments because you or your partner lose your job or fall ill, the golden rule is to inform your lender straightaway. Most lenders will be reasonably sympathetic at least for a while. High street lenders have the reputation of being more helpful than 'centralised' loan companies. If you have a mortgage protection policy, inform your insurer as soon as possible.

Never hand in your keys assuming you can then walk away from your debts — you can't. Even after your home has been repossessed, the lender can pursue you for the money you owe for up to 12 years. Try to co-operate with your lender, and you have a much better chance of keeping your home.

More information

You can seek help from your local Citizen's Advice Bureau or Money Advice Centre. Look in the telephone directory for their numbers.

The National Debtline, tel: 0121-359 8501, specialises in advice and information on housing and other debts.

Where can you go if the high street lenders shut the door in your face?

Banks and building societies aren't always terribly welcoming if you have a less than perfect credit history. But there are plenty of other lenders around who will greet you with outstretched arms.

The problem is they'll more than likely charge you excessive rates of interest and tie you in with high redemption penalties and compulsory insurances. This won't be the case if you knock on Kensington Mortgage Company's door. We may not be a high street giant but we are by far

0800 11 10 20

the largest lender in the UK that can offer mortgages to those who don't fit the mould. Which explains why last year alone, we lent £300 million to people the high street lenders turned away. So don't let a backstreet lender walk all over you. Call us now for more information on 0800 11 10 20.

Kensington
Mortgage Company
Treating people as individuals

7

Best ways to borrow money

Sensible borrowing forms part of most people's financial planning. But the plethora of credit options available can be confusing.

Few families have a strong enough cash flow to cope with making all their major purchases out of income or savings, so identifying the best way to borrow is essential if you don't want to end up paying over the odds for your credit purchases.

Borrowing options

If you do have savings, it will generally make sense to use them rather than take out a loan, because the interest you will earn on your savings is less than you will have to pay on borrowings especially as savings interest is taxed.

To work out which type of credit is most suitable, you need to think about how much you want to borrow, for how long, and how much repayment flexibility you would like.

If you need short-term credit, to cover a cash emergency, for instance, your best bet is probably an authorised overdraft. For small purchases, where convenience and flexibility over payment are at a premium, go for a credit card. Avoid if you can, 'weekly collected credit' where annual interest rates can legitimately top 1000 per cent. Also be wary of 'free credit' from catalogues. You pay for this in prices that are generally higher than local stores or in a lower quantity of the goods you buy.

You may consider a personal loan where repayments are spread over periods of six months to five years for more expensive purchases such as a new car, and for amounts of £10,000 or over, the cheapest way to borrow is normally by taking out a loan secured on your home. But remember your home is at risk if you fail to keep up the repayments and 'consolidation' second mortgage companies can be especially tough.

Counting the cost of credit

It is not easy to compare the true cost of different kinds of borrowing. The law requires lenders to quote Annual Percentage Rates or APRs on most types of loan. APRs take into account the flat interest rate, the amount borrowed and additional costs.

Banks are not forced by law to quote APRs on current account overdrafts. Many now quote an EAR or Equivalent Annual Rate instead — make sure you check on what other charges are levied.

Short-term borrowings

Credit cards are a very flexible and easy way to borrow. You can use them simply as a convenient payment method, and pay your bill in full at the end of each month, which with some cards will give you up to eight weeks' free credit, or you can spread the cost of purchases over several months. You can pay as much or as little as you want each month, subject to a minimum, usually 5 per cent of your balance, or £5. Many still levy an annual fee of £10–12 but there are many banks with no fee for you to avoid this.

But the rates of interest are quite high if you continuously run a debt on your card. It's worth shopping around for the cheapest interest rate — you don't have to take the card offered by your own bank. Switching to a new card can help. You may get a low 'introductory' rate for up to a year. But don't take advantage of this and go on a spending spree or you will be worse off than before!

Store cards work very much like credit cards, but can only be used in one chain of shops. With the honourable exceptions of John Lewis and Marks & Spencer, which offer good rates, these are best avoided. Many charge very high interest rates.

Stores also offer interest-free credit deals on selected items — naturally, these are a very good idea, though you will normally have to put down a deposit, and the repayment times on quite major purchases can be as short as six months.

Arranging an overdraft on your current account is a flexible and convenient way to borrow for shorter periods. But it is not necessarily any cheaper than using a credit card or cheap store card, and you need to watch out for fees and charges. Be careful not to slip into the red inadvertently, or to exceed an agreed overdraft limit.

Interest rates on unauthorised overdrafts are high — and so are other charges.

Longer-term loans

Personal loans from banks or building societies can be a good way to finance larger purchases such as a car, where you need to borrow the money for a longer period.

It can be worth checking whether you can get an interest-free credit deal from a shop or dealer before you borrow. If there is, and you do not need credit, demand a discount for cash.

Personal loans normally set a fixed rate of interest for the term of your loan. This can help you budget, but if interest rates fall, you could lose out. The longer the period you choose to repay the loan, the lower your monthly repayments, but the more you pay overall. And the larger the amount you borrow, generally speaking, the lower the interest rate.

Watch out for whether there are any early repayment penalties. Lenders can charge you for some of the interest payments they have lost because you have settled the loan before its time. You don't have to take a personal loan from the bank or building society where you have your current account. You can go elsewhere to get a better deal.

Secured loans may be suitable for major expenditures like home improvements. They work like personal loans except that they are secured against your home, and your home is at risk if you default on the payments. On the other hand, they are usually cheaper than personal loans, and if you borrow from your mortgage lender, they can be added to your home loan, giving you longer to repay.

You may have to pay for an arrangement fee and for a valuation on your property.

Credit insurance

Lenders often offer you payment protection insurance to cover your repayments if you lose your job or become ill. It is usually offered as part of a specific loan package, so you can't normally shop around for your own insurance. Look over your loan application form carefully, because some lenders automatically charge you for credit cover unless you tick a box saying you *don't* want it.

As with all types of insurance, go through the small print with a fine-tooth comb. Most credit protection insurance runs out after one or two years only, and may not cover your full repayments. There are often deferral periods of one to three months before the policy comes into operation, so it won't totally shield you from the possibility of running up arrears. And it is unlikely to cover you if you take voluntary redundancy. Costs can be as high as £50 for a £500 loan over one year, so it is worthwhile weighing up whether you really need the cover.

Joint borrowings

If you run your finances jointly with your husband or partner, you may decide to have your borrowings in both your names. It is vital that you are aware of where this leaves you if things go wrong. Under the law, it does not matter who actually spent the money, or whose idea it was to take out the loan — what matters are the terms and conditions of the account.

With credit cards, you cannot have a joint account. The principal account holder can give a card to a secondary holder to use, but she or he remains responsible for all the spending.

If you take out a loan in joint names, you are 'jointly and severally liable' with your husband or partner. That means the lender can enforce the full amount of the debt on both or either of you. It makes no difference if the money was used to buy a new car for your husband or your boyfriend — if you have signed, you can be chased for the full debt.

The same applies to joint current accounts with overdraft facilities — you can be held responsible, whether or not it was you who did the spending. It is not unknown for current accounts to be cleared out totally by one partner.

If you separate from your husband or partner, contact your bank and other lenders straight away. Any account which gives them the facility for more borrowing, for instance a credit card where you are the principal holder or an overdraft facility, should be frozen immediately.

The risks of joint borrowing go much further than just having your current account cleaned out, unfortunately. You can lose your home and be saddled with debts running into tens of thousands of pounds if you take bigger loans jointly with your husband, or if you guarantee loans he has taken out.

Small businessmen often ask their wives to put up the family home as collateral for a loan to back their enterprise. But be very careful before you sign for a loan which puts your home at risk.

Always get independent legal advice first. But no matter how good your lawyer or other adviser, any joint venture must depend on relationships.

Bad references

There is nothing to stop you applying for credit in your own right — married women do not need their husband's permission.

It is against the law for lenders to discriminate against women when granting credit, either directly or indirectly, for instance by refusing loans to part-time workers, who are mainly female.

Most lenders use a system called credit scoring to decide whether or not to grant you a loan. As part of the process, most lenders use information from credit reference agencies.

Contrary to popular myth, credit reference agencies do not keep blacklists. But they do store information from the electoral roll, previous credit accounts and county court judgements for debt. They can discriminate against women, not on sex grounds, but because women are lower paid and are more likely to have times of no earnings for family reasons.

If you are turned down for credit, you can ask the lender whether they used credit reference agency information, and for the agency's name and address. You can then apply in writing to the agency, enclosing a £2 fee, and ask for any information held about you. If it is incorrect, you can have it put right.

The lender may reconsider your application in the light of incorrect credit reference agency information. But they are not obliged to — lending money is a commercial decision, and you have no right to credit. You also have no right to be told why your application has been refused although some will.

Bad debts incurred by your husband or a partner who lives or has lived with you may count against you when you apply for a loan, even if you had nothing to do with the borrowings and the relationship is over. In some cases, the activities of your adult children will affect your credit score if they have debts in their own right.

If there is information on your credit reference agency file about people with whom you now have no connection, you should write to the agency and request a notice of disassociation, preventing the agency from giving the information out to lenders.

Dealing with debt

Be honest with yourself if you are running into debt difficulty. Trying to ignore the problem will only make matters worse. Then draw up a plan of campaign. If the situation has not gone too far, you may be able to retrieve it yourself by cutting down on expenses and trying to increase your income.

Draw up a weekly budget and try to identify any areas where you can trim your outgoings. Check whether you may qualify for any benefits, and explore possibilities such as taking in a lodger.

But if that is not enough, inform lenders immediately. Remember that your mortgage or rent and fuel bills are priority debts, so concentrate on them first.

Don't be afraid to seek specialist help. Always seek advice before agreeing to 'consolidate' all your loans in one package. You may be 'jumping out of the frying pan and into the fire'. The loan seller collects a large commission and has no legal duty to give you 'best advice'.

Sources of aid include:

- Money advice centres run by local authorities. Look in your telephone directory or ask at the town hall.
- National Debtline, tel: 0121-359 8501.
- Citizen's Advice Bureaux. Look in your telephone book for details of your local CAB.
- If you feel you have fallen victim to a 'loan shark', contact your local trading standards department. Look in the telephone book for their number.

More information

The Office of Fair Trading will deal with complaints if you feel a credit reference agency has treated you unfairly. It also publishes a leaflet, *Debt, A Survival Guide*. Contact:

OFT
Head Office
Field House
15-25 Bream Building
London EC4A 1PR
Tel: 0171-211 8000

8
Planning a rich retirement

It's easy to put off thinking about your pension — when you're busy working, and perhaps looking after a family too, retirement seems a long way off. But all women should give serious thought to providing for life after work.

The hard fact is that women are still second-class citizens when it comes to retirement and pensions. And the government has increased the state pension age for women but not for men.

A recent report by a leading insurance company found women are much more likely than men to suffer unnecessarily from financial pressures once they give up work.

The survey uncovered worrying trends. Because women usually put their families' immediate financial needs first instead of prioritising their own pension, they are placing themselves at a major disadvantage in retirement. Millions of women are in danger of joining an underclass of low income pensioners reliant entirely on the state to support them.

Female workers have several in-built disadvantages in the building up of a good pension. The first is that, because women still on average only earn around 80 per cent as much as their male colleagues, they either do not pay or cannot afford to pay as much into a pension.

The second is that most women take career breaks to bring up children or care for elderly relatives — time during which they cannot make contributions to a pension fund. Thirdly, many women work part time, and may not be eligible to join a company pension scheme, although recent court decisions have improved the standing of part-time workers — only a third of working women are members of an employers' scheme, compared with almost half the male workforce. However, a recent ruling in the European Court of Justice can mean that a woman excluded from a pension scheme as a result of sex discrimination may be able to join and claim pension credits.

In the past, women relied on their husbands to provide. But this option is no longer tenable. One in three marriages end up in the divorce courts, leaving an ex-wife with no automatic right to a share in her former husband's retirement nest-egg. And most women outlive their husbands, in which case they may be forced to eke out an existence on a much reduced widow's pension.

It all sounds deeply gloomy, not to mention unfair. The good news, though, is that all contributions you can afford to pay into a pension plan are allowed against your Income Tax bill, and by planning ahead and taking responsibility for your own independent pension, you should be able to build yourself a man-sized retirement income.

This chapter and the ones that follow look at pensions from the state, employers and private retirement schemes.

Working women should join a company scheme if they can, and if not, take out a personal pension plan from an insurance company, bank or building society. Full-time wives and mums who do not work outside the home cannot pay into a pension plan, but they should try to build up other savings for retirement. And the earlier you start, the easier — and cheaper — it will be.

Pensions from the state

You are probably entitled to much less from the state than you might imagine. The basic weekly state pension for a single person in 1998/9 is £64.90 or £103.60 for a married couple. Up-to-date rates are listed in leaflet NI196, available from the Benefits Agency.

To qualify for these amounts, however, you must have paid or been credited with National Insurance contributions for roughly nine-tenths of what is still regarded as a standard working life — 44 years for a woman, and 49 years for a man.

Government figures show that in 1992 only 38 per cent of women receiving a state pension were doing so on their own record, not on their husband's. And according to separate figures, in 1991 only 15 per cent of women qualified for a full basic state pension on their own record, compared with nearly 70 per cent of men. Those figures should improve in time, although slowly, as more women become and remain active in the labour force.

- If you have been employed and paid NI contributions for between a quarter and nine-tenths of your working life, you may be entitled to a reduced state pension.
- Married women who have never worked may be entitled to a pension based on their husband's National Insurance contributions, worth about 60 per cent of what he gets. But you have to wait until your husband reaches 65 before it is paid, and you must be aged 60 or more. If you are under 60, your husband can still claim the extra, but it is called an Adult Dependency Addition. DSS leaflet (A13) NI1 *National Insurance for Married Women* has more detail.
- Many women retiring now have paid a reduced rate of NI contribution, often called the 'married woman's stamp'. This option was withdrawn in 1978, but women who had already taken it were allowed to continue. Unfortunately, reduced rate contributions do not count towards a state pension of your own. If you have never paid anything other than the married woman's stamp you must rely on your husband's contributions for a married couple's pension. You might consider electing to pay full NI contributions now if you are still paying reduced rate. Ask the DSS to state the advantages and drawbacks of this.

Home Responsibilities Protection

Women — and men — who have to stay at home to look after children, an elderly relative or a disabled dependant can safeguard their basic state pension rights by claiming Home Responsibilities Protection. If you are not already receiving HRP you can claim at your local Benefits Agency.

State Earnings Related Pension Scheme (SERPS)

SERPS is paid on top of your basic State pension to those in the plan. It is compulsory for all employees earning more than a minimum amount unless they are 'contracted out'. Two large groups are contracted out of SERPS — most of those in company schemes and those with 'appropriate personal pensions'. It is worked out on earnings since 1978 on which you have paid National Insurance contributions. You pay NI contributions on earnings between an upper and a lower weekly limit — in 1998/9 these limits are £64 and £485 respectively. Because of the rising costs of SERPS, the government is downgrading the benefits from the scheme so the most you will receive is falling from a quarter of the average of your best 20 years' earnings to a fifth of the average of your lifetime earnings. This affects those retiring after 2000.

The change to lifetime earnings instead of the best 20 years is particularly damaging to women's prospects of a good SERPS pension, because career breaks caring for children and periods of part-time work will reduce the total average earnings figure. The self-employed are not eligible for a SERPS pension.

Many women are contracted out of SERPS through their company scheme. They are entitled to a guaranteed minimum pension which is roughly the same as what they would have received under SERPS.

A large number of younger women have contracted out through a special personal pension from an insurance company. Contracting out is explained in more detail later in the book. The future of SERPS is in doubt following the Government's announcement of its intention to launch new style 'stakeholder' pensions. Existing SERPS benefits will be protected.

Equal pension ages

The Government is planning to raise the State pension age for women from 60 to 65, the same as for men, by the year 2020.

Equalisation of pension ages will be phased in over ten years starting in April 2010. Only those born after 6 April 1955 will have to wait right up until 65. Women born before 6 April 1950 will not be affected and will still be able to draw their state pension at age 60. Those born between 1950 and 1955 will have their State pension age delayed proportionally.

More information

If you have any questions or worries about your state pension, contact your local Benefits Agency.

For a forecast of your state pension, fill in form BR19 from your local Benefits Agency. If there are gaps in your contribution record, you may be able to make them up by paying extra voluntary contributions now.

9

A pension with your job

It is usually an excellent idea to join a company pension scheme if you can. You receive tax relief at your highest rate on all the contributions you make, and your nest-egg grows tax free. You will also benefit from contributions made by your employer and this can often be worth far more than your own contributions. You could lose this if you opt out.

Company pensions are moving slowly towards equality of the sexes. The good side of this is that more schemes are allowing part-time employees, most of whom are women, to join. The downside is that most schemes have now moved to equal pension ages for men and women, usually any time between 60 and 65.

Many people have become worried about the safety of company pension schemes after the late Robert Maxwell was discovered to have plundered millions from company pension funds. The vast majority of schemes, however, are well-run and secure, and there is a new Pensions Act. This contains a series of measures to improve the safety of pension funds. Do not be deterred by the Maxwell scandal — it is highly unlikely to happen to you.

Pension contributions from staff and employers are channelled into a pension fund, which is quite separate from the company you work for. It is run by trustees, who are responsible for managing the fund and making sure pensioners and their families receive the benefits they have been promised.

There are three main types of company pension. It is rare for employees to be offered a choice between schemes — you normally have to take the type your company offers.

Final salary schemes

These are the most common arrangement. Final salary schemes promise to pay a pension based on a proportion of what you are earning on retirement. The proportion depends on how many years you have worked for the company. Most schemes pay a pension of 1/60th or 1/80th of final salary for every year's service. So if, for instance, Joanna has worked for her company for 20 years, and is a member of a 1/60th scheme, she would receive a pension of 20/60 or one-third of her final salary. The maximum pension you can receive is two-thirds of your final salary. When you finally retire, you are allowed to take part of your pension as a tax-free lump sum. If you work in the public sector or local government, teaching, for example, the pension fraction is 1/80th with a tax-free lump sum in addition.

Company schemes also provide benefits for your dependants if you die. Widowers' pensions are normally a proportion of your pension, whether you die after retiring or in service. If you die in service, your husband and/or family may receive a death benefit, with a maximum of four times your salary.

Typically, you will be asked to contribute around 5 per cent of your salary although some schemes are 'free'. Your company will pay in the extra money needed to cover the cost of your benefits.

Money Purchase Schemes

These have become more popular over recent years as they enable employers to limit their costs and avoid the 'open-ended' bill they could be forced to pay with 'guaranteed' final salary pensions, as well as some Pensions Act obligations. Contributions from members and the employer are paid into a fund, often run by an insurance company, which invests the money in stocks, shares, property and government bonds. The pension you will receive is not determined in advance — it depends on the performance of the fund's investments, and on the cost of buying an annuity to provide an income when you retire.

As with a final salary scheme, you can take part of your pension as a tax-free lump sum, and benefits for dependants are often provided.

Executive Pension Plans (EPPs)

If you are lucky enough to be in a senior position, an EPP from a life insurance company could enable your employer — your own company if you are a director/shareholder — to put large sums into a plan and claim tax relief. The rules are now very complex and EPPs require expert advice. The 'executive' can claim tax relief on her contributions.

10

Personal pension plans

Women who are unable to join a company pension scheme because there is none or they are self-employed should consider taking out a personal pension. This works like a money purchase scheme, with your contributions going into an investment pot which is turned into retirement benefits when you stop work.

Personal plans are available from insurance companies, banks and building societies. As with company pensions, any payments you make receive tax relief at your highest rate. So a 23 per cent taxpayer who is an employee would need to pay only £77 to make a contribution worth £100. Self-employed women would pay the full £100 and claim back the tax relief via their tax assessment.

Because of the tax benefits, the Inland Revenue sets limits on the contributions you can make. Women — and men — under 35 can pay up to 17.5 per cent of earnings into a personal pension. For ages 36 to 45, the maximum is 20 per cent; for ages 46 to 50, it is 25 per cent; for ages 51 to 55, it is 30 per cent; for ages 56 to 60 it is 35 per cent and for over 60s it is 40 per cent.

Most employers will not make contributions to a personal pension, and you normally have to pay extra for death benefits and dependants' pensions provided free by company schemes.

However, some employers do contribute to so-called group personal pension plans as an alternative to running a company pension scheme. Frequently they add on death in service benefits at no cost to you.

Choosing a personal pension is not easy, and you may wish to consult an independent financial adviser. He or she should be able to give you more information about the plans, and help you pick one from a reputable company with a good performance record and low costs. Many pension providers offer a 'career break'. But some of these penalise women and men who take advantage of it. You need to ask questions. If you are uncertain, ask for a 'recurring single premium' plan rather than a 'regular premium' plan. *Money Management* magazine provides regular in-depth surveys.

You can take out more than one personal pension, which reduces the risk of putting all your money into a poor performer. But that means paying more than one set of start-up charges. With any personal pension, you have to pay set-up charges and an annual management fee, but these can vary from plan to plan. You cannot draw the benefits of a personal pension until you are aged 50, but the longer you leave it, the better the pension you will eventually receive.

Lower paid women are at a disadvantage with personal pensions, because if you can only afford small payments, much of your contributions may be eaten up by charges. But if you are an employee, you still receive tax relief on your contributions of 23 per cent, even if you do not earn enough to pay tax, or you pay at the lower 20 per cent rate. However, the reality is that few if any non-taxpayers can afford to lock up money until their retirement age.

There are three main ways to invest in a personal pension plan. Which you choose depends on how old you are, and how much investment risk you are prepared to take in the hope of earning a bigger pension.

With-profits plans

These are a relatively safe bet. With-profits pensions guarantee you a basic sum on retirement. That guaranteed sum is increased each year as bonuses are added. The bonuses depend on the investment performance of the pension fund you are investing in. Once added, they cannot be taken away. When your plan matures, a final bonus is also added. With-profits plans are suitable for women who do not want to take a big risk with their retirement money.

Unit-linked plans

With a unit-linked plan, your contributions are invested in a fund linked to the stock market. The value of the fund rises and falls in line with share values, and what you receive at the end depends on how well it performs. Unit-linked plans are more risky than with-profits, but they offer the chance of bigger rewards over the long term although they have often failed to do so. They are suitable for younger women, and those prepared to take more risk in the hope of more gain. Normally you will be advised to switch out of a unit-linked plan into with-profits or a deposit about five years before you are due to retire, so you won't be hit if there is a stock market crash just before you stop work.

Deposit plans

These are the safest option of all. Deposit-based personal pensions are just like bank and building society savings accounts. Your capital is guaranteed not to fall in value, and interest is added at regular intervals. But these are only a good bet if you are either highly opposed to taking any risk, or have five years or fewer to go to retirement. Over longer periods, they are likely to do much worse than with-profits or unit-linked plans, because inflation eats into the value of your capital.

Contracting out of SERPS

There are also special personal pension plans designed for people who want to contract out of SERPS. The reason you may wish to contract out is that you might achieve better benefits privately than through the state scheme.

You may automatically be contracted out of SERPS through an employer's scheme in which case you have little choice, or you may choose to contract out yourself.

If you are contracted out through a final salary scheme, you cannot do any worse than with SERPS. If you contract out privately, rather than through a final pay scheme, you could do better than SERPS, or you could do worse. Your Non-SERPS pension will depend on investment criteria and costs. It cannot be guaranteed.

You contract out privately by opening a specialised personal pension plan from an insurance company. You do not have to pay anything — the money comes from part of your employer's and your National Insurance contributions. These are transferred into your personal pension plan.

Whether or not it makes sense to contract out of SERPS yourself depends mainly on your age and how much you earn as costs on plans from women on lower earnings can eat up contributions. It is safer for women who earn less than £9000 to £10000 a year and are aged over 35 to stay in SERPS. Women under 35 on higher earnings should consider contracting out if they are sure they will be working for the next two years and paying contributions into their personal pension. These age limits can change with different pension providers and at different times. Always seek advice from a finance professional before making up your mind.

If you are contracted out, you can contract back in again when you get older or if your earnings drop. It is a yearly decision. This will depend on your age and salary and the exact nature of the Government incentive to contract out. You cannot draw your contracted-out SERPS pension until you reach state pension age.

More information

If you have a problem or complaint with a company or personal pension that cannot be resolved to your satisfaction, contact:

The Occupational Pensions Advisory Service
11 Belgrave Road
London SW1V 1RB
Tel: 0171-233 8080

If they cannot resolve the problem, they will pass your complaint to the Pensions Ombudsman.

Pensions

One of the great ironies of attitudes towards money in this country is that while men seem happily to be taking on the traditional female role of shopper, many women appear much less keen to become involved in financial decision-making. Appearances aren't everything, of course, but compare the numbers of men flocking through the doors of your local Marks & Spencer store and the numbers of women who express confidence in their ability to understand what is on offer financially and to make the right decisions - such as taking out loans or arranging pensions.

Recent research for Marks & Spencer Financial Services, for instance, has shown that while 62% of men claim to have a good understanding of pensions, only 49% of women claim the same.*

(Of course the key here may well be that word "claim" - believing you understand and actually understanding are two very different things, so perhaps numbers of men and women who actually understand about pensions is about the same!)

There is a generally held perception that pensions are difficult to understand; and this is hardly surprising when one considers some of the worst examples of jargon and "small print" which have beset the industry in the past.

The result of this lack of confidence combined with the complexity of some pensions is made worse by the fact that a significant number of women - around 13% according to M&SFS research - believe that a personal pension or an occupational pension is irrelevant or unnecessary for them.*

The same survey showed that while 20% of the women questioned had a personal pension, only 16% had an occupational pension. These figures compare with 29% and 31% respectively of the men questioned. These figure back up the well documented fact that far fewer women than men have adequate pension arrangements in place.*

Given this background of a lack of confidence and under-provision, how can a Marks & Spencer Pension help?

For a start, as you would expect from Marks & Spencer, our pensions offer quality, good value for money, and security - ours is a name you can trust to look after you and your pension.

The Independent newspaper recently conducted a review of pensions across all providers to give direct comparisons. They used a system suggested by the Office of Fair Trading with ratings from A+ down to C-, that take into account charges, transfer values and the proportion of people who decide not to continue with a chosen plan.

The Marks & Spencer Personal Pension Plan scored A+AA+, one of the top two in the country.**

So, just as you know that the food, clothing and goods for your home that you buy at Marks & Spencer will all be of the same high quality, you can be sure that our pensions have to comply with regulatory standards.

We keep things simple. We offer only two pension plans, and all the information about them is designed to be straightforward and easy to understand.

We also keep things flexible so that your pension plan can change as your life changes - without loading on extra charges every time you alter the details. You can, for example, stop and start, increase or decrease contributions at any time without being penalised. And if you do decide to stop your contributions, either temporarily or permanently, we won't charge the monthly plan fee.

This is particularly important for women, whose working life pattern can change dramatically if they choose to have children.

In an ideal world, the majority of women might want to move from full time career development to a mix of maternity break, part time or full time working while their family is growing. Our view is that personal pensions should reflect this natural progression.

Our pensions are easily adaptable to whatever lifestyle pattern suits the individual; we know that you are likely to change job, have children, work part-time or change career - and we don't penalise you for leading a perfectly normal life.

So we build flexibility into our two pensions plans.

Our first, the Marks & Spencer Personal Pension Plan, is for people who are in work but are not in a company pension scheme, including those who are self-employed.

The second, the Marks & Spencer Supplementary Pension Plan, is for people who are already paying into a company scheme but who want to top it up with another scheme. (This kind of pension is also called a Free Standing Additional Voluntary Contribution or FSAVC.)

While designed for different employment situations, the pensions share many features - starting with the fact that you can contribute as little as £30 a month, with an option for automatic increases of 5% or 10%.

Charging structures are often the most complex part of a pension to understand and often this complexity masks high charges which can have a debilitating effect on the long-term viability of a pension.

But a Marks & Spencer pension has a clear charging structure, with no hidden surprises. Not only are they very straightforward to understand, they are highly competitive; in the Personal Investment Authority report "Life Assurance Disclosure: Three Years On", published in January 1998, Marks & Spencer Personal Pension Plan was ranked as one of the top two products in the industry.***

Once you have taken out a pension, we won't penalise you if you decide to increase or decrease your contributions or stop them temporarily or permanently. (If you do decide to stop we won't charge you the monthly plan fee.)

We have a low annual management charge which, in particular, benefits long-term investors. The rate is 0.75% in years one to 10, but drops to 0.5% after that. And we don't impose any charges if, for any reason, you decide to transfer you pension.

Taking the fear factor out of buying a pension has been one of our key aims. And the best way to do that is to give good, clear information.

We do not employ staff on a sales commission basis. They are friendly and knowledgeable people who are on hand to help you by providing all the information you need to decide for yourself if a Marks & Spencer Pension is right for you.

While some in the pensions industry allow only a 14-day "cooling off" period, Marks & Spencer Financial Services offers the maximum period allowed - a full 30 days - during which you can change your mind.

Our expert staff can answer your questions and give you practical assistance. They cannot give you their opinion on other companies' pensions or give you specific advice on your final choice - but they will tell you if they feel you should consult an independent financial adviser.

When you ask us for more details about Marks & Spencer Pensions, we will send you an information pack. However because of the two kinds of pensions we offer, and the different needs of our customers, the information we send out will vary.

The questions we ask will help us to make sure that we send you information that is relevant to your needs. For example, the answer you give us will allow us to work out which of our two pensions you are eligible for.

We ask when you want to retire and how much you would like to contribute to your pension, so that we can prepare a Personal Illustration for you. This will show you howmuch your Marks & Spencer Pension could be worth when you retire.

And if you are an employee, we ask for your salary details so that we can make sure that the pension contributions you plan to make do not exceed Inland Revenue limits.

Our staff will be happy to guide you through the questions; and of course the call is free when you dial 0800 363428.

To give you an idea of how much you could expect to pay for your pension, a woman of 25 who wants to retire at 55 with an annual pension of £15,000 would need to pay £125.81 a month into a Marks & Spencer Personal Pension Plan.

A woman of 35 who wants to retire at 60 with an annual pension of £15,000 would need to pay £184.17 a month into a Marks & Spencer Personal Pension Plan.

All in all, Marks & Spencer pensions are designed to help today's busy woman, at work or at home, to make informed decisions about her future.

Please remember that the value of your investment is not guaranteed and can go down as well as up.

- All figures quoted are on a gross basis.
- These figures are only examples and are not guaranteed - they are not minimum or maximum amounts.
- You could get back more or less than this.
- All insurance companies use the same rate of growth (9%) for illustrations but their charges vary. They also use the same rate to show how funds may be converted into pension income (7.5%).
- Do not forget that inflation would reduce what you could buy in the future with the amount shown.
- Your pension income will depend on how your investments grow and interest rates at the time you retire.
- We believe that customers want to make up their own minds about our Plans so we do not offer advice, but can provide factual information about any of our products. If you require advice, please contact an authorised financial adviser.

Marks and Spencer Financial Services Limited
Regulated by the Personal Investment Authority
Registered Office: Michael House,
Baker Street, London W1A 1DN
Registered in England No 1772585
A subsidiary of Marks and Spencer plc

Marks and Spencer Financial Services Limited represents only the Marks & Spencer Financial Services Marketing Group for the sale of life assurance, pensions and also unit trust and associated personal equity plan products.

* Source: BRMB November November 1997 for Marks & Spencer Financial Services, using a 962 sample size
** Source: The Independent, 13 December 1997
*** Source: Personal Investment Authority report "Life Assurance Disclosure: Three Years on" January 1998

11

Building a man-sized pension

It's very important for working women to pump up their pensions while they can. There are three good reasons for this: first, most women need to make up for career breaks, second, many women in future will want to retire 'early', before they reach 65; third, because women live longer than men on average, those with a personal pension or money purchase company scheme receive a lower annual pension than a man the same age. This is because women live longer than men. The money you build up in a personal pension is used to buy an annuity from an insurance company. Annuity rates are lower for women because insurers expect to have to pay out for longer.

Women who have left pension planning until their late thirties or beyond should make a big effort to boost their pension as soon as possible.

What happens to my pension during a career break?

The most important difference between men and women when it comes to pension planning is that women have to plan to make up for lost time spent looking after the family. Before you can start to plan, though, you need to know your pension rights while you are away from work.

State pension

If you are receiving Statutory Maternity Pay (SMP) you are credited with National Insurance contributions towards your state pension.

Company pension

Is is illegal, under European law, to exclude women from pension schemes. This includes a ban on excluding women who take maternity leave. Company pension schemes treat time off work to have children whilst you are receiving SMP as pensionable service. Most insist you continue to pay your contributions to the scheme as a percentage of SMP, rather than a percentage of your salary.

If you take more time off after your SMP stops, it is not normally counted for pension benefits. Some schemes may treat you as having left when your SMP stops and rejoining as a new member when you go back to work. That reduces your pension on retirement.

Personal pensions

During any time you are off work and not receiving pay, you cannot make payments to a personal pension plan. Nor will any money be credited to a personal plan to contract out of SERPS, because you are not making any National Insurance contributions. When you go back to work, you can start to pay into your personal pension again. You may wish to do so at a higher rate to make up for lost time, provided this is within the limits and you can afford them.

Full-time wives and mothers

Women who do not carry out any paid work outside the home are not allowed to pay into a pension plan. But it is still important to build up your own independent retirement nest-egg if you can afford to — or can persuade a partner with money to help you out. One useful method, again if you have the money, is to buy a Personal Equity Plan or the new Individual Savings Account (from April 1999). Although you do not get tax relief on money put in, there is no tax to pay on money taken out. And a PEP is far more flexible than a pension. The chapters on savings and investments earlier in this book give more detail.

Boosting your pension

If you are a member of a company pension scheme you can make additional voluntary contributions (AVCs) to the scheme itself or free standing AVCs (FSAVCs) to an insurance company fund. The most you can pay into a company scheme and AVCs or FSAVCs together is 15 per cent of your total salary each tax year. AVCs of either sort can only be used to boost your pension income, not to enhance the tax-free lump sum the Inland Revenue allows you to take when you retire.

Using additional voluntary contributions to spice up your retirement savings is highly tax-efficient. Like your normal payments into a pension scheme, AVCs and FSAVCs attract tax relief at your highest rate, so a £100 payment would really only cost a basic rate taxpayer £77 and a higher rate taxpayer £60. And once invested, your extra contributions are allowed to grow almost entirely free of gains tax and income tax.

AVCs or FSAVCs?

AVCs are Additional Voluntary Contributions; FSAVCs are Free Standing AVCs. Both enable you to buy a boost to your pension via extra cash into a fund. There is a limit on how much you can put into a fund. This is determined by calculating 15 per cent of your annual earnings and then subtracting your contribution — but not that of your employer —- to the company scheme. If you already contribute 6 per cent, your AVC or FSAVC could go up to 9 per cent, for instance. Your decision is an annual one. Normally your contributions are invested — and don't forget risk factors — to produce a fund at retirement which you turn into extra pension although a few schemes let you buy 'added years' so your final pension assumes you have worked longer for that employer than you did.

Before you sign up, check on what benefits the AVCs will provide. As a rule of thumb the charges on AVCs are likely to be lower than on FSAVCs, but you have no control over how the money is invested.

You can buy FSAVCs from insurance companies, banks, building societies, unit trusts, friendly societies and a couple of investment trusts. The charges will probably be higher, but you have a much wider choice of investments. FSAVCs are generally less popular.

Personal pensions

Women who have taken out a personal pension plan cannot make AVCs or FSAVCs. But you can increase your retirement fund simply by bumping up your contributions.

You can choose to pay extra to your main plan, or start a new one if you wish. But if you start afresh, you may run into a new set of expensive upfront fees.

Early retirement

Many women dream of retiring early, a trend that is likely to grow with the raising of younger women's pension age to 65. Only 12 per cent of women have taken any action to make up the shortfall so they would still be able to retire at age 60.

Early retirement is expensive. Not only will you have to wait for your state pension, but you will also get a lower company or personal pension. That's because you have paid in fewer contributions, your pension fund has had less time to grow and your pension provider will have to pay you an income for more years.

So if you do want to retire early, the advice on boosting your pension contributions and other savings as much as you can applies even more.

We can help you gain pounds

Planning for your future financial well-being may seem like a daunting task. But it needn't be.

The sooner you sit down and plan ahead, the easier it becomes to achieve your goals.

This is where Barclays Life can help. As the life and pensions arm of the Barclays Group, you can rest assured that we have both the resources and depth of experience to provide professional and tailored advice you can trust to meet your needs.

To this end, we employ over 700 specialist financial advisers throughout the UK who are qualified to look at your protection, investment and pension planning requirements. They can put together solutions that are practical and affordable. And they can do so at any time or location that is convenient for you.

So if your financial affairs aren't quite as healthy as you'd like, call Barclays Life today on 0800 100 171, and we'll propose a sensible plan that will allow you to gain pounds and stay financially fit.

BARCLAYS LIFE

GET REAL ABOUT YOUR FUTURE

All through our working lifetime the money we earn pays the bills. What plans have you made to ensure your income does not stop when you cash your last pay cheque?

Research conducted by Barclays Life, the pensions and life assurance arm of the Barclays Group, has revealed the harsh reality that nearly 40% of all women have no pension other than the State entitlement. Some of those women may receive little more than the basic State pension for a single person, which currently amounts to a meagre £64.70[1] a week. If you were retiring today and did not have a company or personal pension, would you want to have to rely on State benefits? Even if you have made arrangements for your retirement, can you be sure that they are adequate?

The message from today's pensioners to our generation is clear – if we want to avoid spending our old age worrying about money and struggling to make ends meet, we need to act now. Having to scrimp and save, or to rely on family in retirement, is no reward for a lifetime of hard work.

When's the best time to start?
When you are in your 20s and 30s, retirement seems in the distant future. But in today's labour market "sell-by dates" seem to be coming closer. We may well see more people having to retire earlier, or work on a part-time basis towards the end of their career. So saving up for when you stop work shouldn't be put off or nudged down the list of priorities; retirement may be closer than you think.

Mary McGrath, Pension Marketing Manager at Barclays Life, says "It's unlikely that many of us thought about retirement when we started our first day at work, but it is absolutely key for women to take pensions seriously. I started my retirement planning in my early 20s because I know I don't want to wait until 65 to retire. After my mortgage it's my next priority."

So if you haven't started your retirement planning yet, there's no time like the present. And even if you have, you may not be giving it the priority it deserves. Barclays Life's research has shown that almost three quarters of women with personal pensions have never increased their monthly contribution, despite the effects of inflation.

To be sure your retirement savings are keeping pace with inflation, you need to check your contributions regularly – and adjust them accordingly.

Putting enough away.
Mary McGrath says; "It's easy to become complacent once you've started your pension, but it's crucial to regularly review your arrangements to ensure you're still putting enough away. I make sure that as my salary increases the contributions to my pension also increase. I'm also really keen to retire at the same time as my husband, so planning our financial future together is a shared objective, particularly as one of us may want a career break at some point."

Clearly, with every year that you wait to review your pension arrangements, the cost of providing for your future will increase.

Monthly contribution required up to retirement to provide:
The chart below shows the initial monthly contribution you will need to make to provide an income at retirement of £750 a month in today's terms.

Starting age next birthday, retiring at 60	Contribution required
25	£255
30	£309
35	£382
40	£485
45	£648

Assumptions:
State benefits and other company or personal pensions have been excluded from this calculation. Annual pension payable from age 60, quarterly in advance to a policyholder during her lifetime only. It is assumed investments will grow at 9% per annum before the deduction of all charges. The pension at age 60 is calculated assuming inflation of 4.5% per annum and an annuity interest rate of 7.5%.

Important notes:
These figures are only illustrative. An assessment of your needs would be necessary before a recommendation could be made. A "Key features" document, including a personal quotation, would be given to you if a recommendation was made.

[1] Rate effective from 6/4/98

These contributions may seem considerable, but you will be using them to secure a regular income for the length of your retirement.

There's nothing wrong with hoping to retire early, or wanting an annual increase to your pension, or looking forward to spending a lump sum on yourself. But to enjoy any of these benefits you must be prepared to put additional funds away now, on top of your provision for that decent standard of living in retirement. Furthermore, you need to review this amount regularly to ensure that it is still enough for the retirement you want.

Mary McGrath

Help with your contributions.

Under current legislation you may claim tax relief on your contributions at potentially the highest rate you pay. So, for example, a basic rate taxpayer will receive up to 23 pence for every £1 contributed, and a higher rate taxpayer will receive up to 40 pence. For employees, the basic rate tax relief is paid directly into your plan. For everyone, it can make the monthly premium look much more manageable.

The funds in which your money is invested are exempt from UK taxation on their capital gains and on income, except for the dividend income received on UK equities. When the time comes to take retirement benefits some plans allow people to kick-off their retirement with a tax-free lump sum. Your pension however will be taxed as earned income.

The values of relief quoted are those currently applicable. The levels and bases of taxation can change. The values of tax reliefs depend upon the circumstances of the individual taxpayer.

What's the right plan for me?

As an employee who receives a pension with your job, you can invest 15 per cent (including any contribution to the scheme you might already make) of what you earn on top of your employer's contributions. You can either make additional contributions to the main scheme or you can set up a free-standing arrangement to run in parallel. You should take advice on which is most suitable; your Barclays Life Adviser can explain all the options.

If you have a personal pension instead of a company pension, you can increase your contributions simply by upping the premiums or by taking out a new plan. The main thing to watch out for is the Inland Revenue's contribution limit, which is a percentage of your earnings that increases as you get older. Your Adviser can give you expert advice on these details – and on which option is most appropriate for you.

If you're one of the four in 10 women who don't have any pension plans apart from that currently provided by the State, then again your Adviser can explain the advantages of starting to save for your retirement today.

Peace of mind for the future.

Barclays Life provides plans which can give you valuable peace of mind by providing an income if you are off work through prolonged illness or injury, or by protecting your loved ones in case the unthinkable should happen and you were to die prematurely. You can arm yourself with an impressive amount of cover for a surprisingly modest outlay. And in so doing you can rest assured that you have taken care of those you love.

The first step is to talk to someone who knows the personal finance market – someone whose advice you can trust as you plan for your retirement and look to protect yourself and those who rely on you. For a free and confidential discussion of your needs, call 0800 100 171 to make an appointment with a Barclays Life Adviser.

Full written details of any of Barclays Life's plans are also available by calling this number. You do not need to be an existing Barclays customer to benefit from this service.

We look forward to hearing from you.

To make sure we maintain a quality service we may monitor or record phone calls.

BARCLAYS LIFE

Barclays Life gives advice and recommendations only on its own products and those of the Barclays Marketing Group. Barclays Life Assurance Company Limited. Head Office: 252-256 Romford Road, Forest Gate, London E7 9JB. United Kingdom. Tel. (0181) 534 5544. Registered in England. Registered number 858511. Registered Office: 54 Lombard Street, London EC3P 3AH. Member of the Association of British Insurers. Regulated by the Personal Investment Authority.

12

Pension tips for job-changers

Pensions are a highly complex area. Matters are made worse because most company pensions assume people do not change their jobs.

Most women do not work for the same employer throughout their career. If you have a personal pension plan, it is portable, so you can continue to pay in even though you switch jobs.

But if you are a member of a company pension scheme, you must decide what to do with the benefits you have built up. If you have been a scheme member for less than two years, you can take a refund of your contributions less tax at 20 per cent and often a deduction for National Insurance. Taking the cash means you miss out on your employer's contribution.

Once you have been a scheme member for two years, you are limited to leaving your pension where it is, switching to a new employer's scheme, or transferring to a personal pension.

Leaving your pension where it is

Your pension rights stay in your former employer's scheme, where they must be increased each year by at least 5 per cent or the rate of inflation, whichever is the lower. When you reach retirement age, you will receive a pension from the scheme.

Moving your pension to a new employer's scheme

You may have the option of transferring your pension rights to your new company's scheme. Your old employer's pension scheme will calculate a 'transfer value' — or cash sum equivalent to the rights you have accumulated. There is no hard and fast formula for working out transfer values, and there has been concern in the pensions industry that some early leavers may get a raw deal. On top of that, your new employer's scheme may place a seemingly low value on your pension rights. But both schemes are supposed to treat you fairly.

Ask for guidance from your new company's pension department. If the sum is large enough, seek professional help from a financial adviser who may decide to employ a consulting actuary.

Transferring your pension to an insurance company

You also have the option of transferring your pension rights to a personal pension plan. This type of transfer has received a great deal of bad publicity after it emerged that many miners, nurses, teachers and other workers had been persuaded by independent financial advisers and insurance company sales-people to transfer out of their occupational schemes into inferior personal pensions, even though they were not changing jobs. The sellers gained high commission payments. City watchdog the Personal Investment Authority has been investigating the 'pensions scandal' for some years and still, few people who were mis-sold plans have received compensation thanks to years of heel-dragging by pensions companies.

The golden rule is: never transfer out of a company scheme into a personal plan if you are not leaving your job. If you have done so, contact the insurance company or financial adviser where you bought your personal pension. You may also wish to approach your trade union for help.

The Pensional Investment Authority is also probing the potential pension losses made by many thousands of job-changers and people made redundant who may have been ill-advised to transfer their rights into personal pensions. The situation here is less clear-cut than that of people who took out a personal plan when they carried on working for the same employer and could have remained a member of the company scheme.

If you are leaving your job, it is only worth transferring to a personal plan if it will provide a better pension in the end. That depends on how well it performs. Insurance companies and

A little

black

number

that will

take you

from work

to play.

The little black phone number

below is all you need for friendly,

helpful advice from our

fully trained Pension Advisers.

Simply, clearly and with no

obligation, they'll help you pick

a pension that suits you now,

and as your circumstances change

- if you move jobs, take a

baby break or want to alter

what you pay, for instance.

Lines are open 8.00am to 10.00pm,

364 days a year. Be smart and

call us on the number below.

SCOTTISH WIDOWS

Looking good for your pension.

Please telephone quoting reference: 288DE08 or talk to your Independent Financial Adviser.

0345 6789 10

advisers have to work out carefully whether transferring is the best advice for you, taking account of the growth needed in the personal plan to match the benefits offered by your company scheme.

It's important to get this decision right — the wrong choice could leave you thousands of pounds out of pocket. So take as much advice as you can. Ask your company scheme for assistance, and consider consulting an independent financial adviser with expertise in the pensions field. There is no hurry to make up your mind — you can transfer your pension rights out of an old scheme at any time.

More information

If you have benefits in old company schemes that you cannot trace, consult:

The Registrar of Pension Schemes
Occupational Pensions Board (OPRA)
PO Box 1NN
Newcastle upon Tyne NE99 1NN
Tel: 0191-225 6393

Flexibility for life

On average, you are likely to change your job every five years – and you may take breaks to raise a family, retrain, or because of redundancy, illness or accident.

Do you know what you are doing tomorrow?

Next week? Next year?

adapt

Lincoln has launched a pension designed to provide security for your future and flexibility for your lifestyle today – whatever your job, whatever your circumstances.

fit

In short, a pension that provides flexibility for life.

change

Find out how a Lincoln pension offers security and flexibility for you, to meet your changing lifestyle and unpredictable future. Contact freephone **0800 7319635** quoting reference FPW – to find out more.

safeguard

A member of Lincoln Financial Group

GIRLS ON TOP

Working women cherish being able to afford life's little luxuries - the Greek getaway once a year or the odd night out with friends, makes it all worthwhile. While women make up just over half of the overall population, 51% (1), they also constitute just under half the employed population, and the time is only around the corner when working women will outnumber working men.

Having a job and a salary is not just about greater independence - it's about more choice. Whether you like it or not, money matters, and more money means having freedom to do what you want to do.

But it takes more than a weekly wage to really go it alone and it's only by carefully organising your finances that you gain greater control over your life. More and more women are taking responsibility for their financial affairs, and are becoming more sophisticated in the financial products they are taking out.

So what does all this mean for you?

It means that, as you no longer have to rely on your partner for housekeeping money, neither should you rely on him to secure your financial future.

Lincoln believes everyone now has the purchasing power to buy whatever financial products suit their needs, whether it's saving for a rainy day, investing for your future or protecting your mortgage, there is something out there for you.

'Financial Planning' covers a whole host of things and certainly isn't as boring as it sounds. Consider it as a way of enabling you to afford to buy what you want to buy and of protecting what's important to you.

It's a fact of life that women need to pay more attention to their finances than men, because they are more likely to work part-time, and take career breaks to start a family. They also receive lower pensions in retirement than men, around one-tenth lower, because they live longer and tend to retire earlier.

There are certain areas where women need to pay particular attention, so here are some tips from Lincoln to make sure you stay on top:

Pensions

Women need to lavish special care on their pension because, with one in three marriages ending in divorce, (an estimated 174,000 couples untied the knot in 1996), more often than not a pension will be all they have to rely on for income in retirement.

Encouragingly, whilst around 9 million working men have some sort of pension provision, there are nearly 6 million women who belong either to an occupational scheme or who have taken out their own pension plan. (2) Yet, considering there are just under 11 million women in employment, (2) this still means that nearly half have no pension provision at all, and this is a situation that women must address.

Every woman should have some sort of pension over and above what the state provides and there are a number of reasons why this is the case:

First and foremost, everyone receives attractive tax breaks when they take out a pension. For every £1 you or your employer contributes, the government will pay in a further 23p or 40p on your behalf, depending on what level tax payer you are.

Secondly, if you don't have your own form of pension provision, you're not going to receive very much by way of income when you retire - it's as simple as that. The basic state pension is just over £62 a week (almost £65 a week from April 1998) for a single person and just under £100 a week (just over £103 from April 1998) for a married couple - could you live comfortably on that?

The amount you will receive from the state top up pension (SERPS) will depend on the number of national insurance contributions you have made. This means that a lot of women who work part time may not clock up enough earnings to qualify for SERPS pay out. To make matters worse, part-timers may not have put in enough hours on the time sheet to qualify for even their company pension scheme.

Women working part-time shouldn't neglect their pension provision. Even if you are not paying tax on your earnings you can still contribute net of basic rate income tax into a personal pension. Remember, retirement is a full-time occupation!

Thirdly, unless you are working you can't pay into a pension. If you take time off to have children you will make a big dent in the size of your pension pot, which will reduce the income you receive when you eventually retire.

For example, a 27 year-old woman paying £100 a month into her personal pension plan, taking four years off to have a child, could reduce her eventual pension by up to £3000 a year. More practically, if you have grown accustomed to two salaries, it will be a dramatic drop if you suddenly have to survive on just one pension when you both retire.

If you are lucky enough to work for a company which provides an employee pension scheme, then join it - in many cases your employer will be paying money into it for you. If it is a final salary scheme, this may be a considerable amount. Consider making additional contributions into it if you can, these will help to boost your benefits.

If your company does not provide a pension or you are self-employed, the next best thing is to take out a personal pension and pay into it on your own. The sooner you start to pay in as much as you can comfortably afford, the better.

Women in particular need flexibility when it comes to choosing a pension. Lincoln recommend that you choose one which allows you to stop payments without penalty if you decide to take a career break or have children, and one which will allow you to reduce payments, if, for example, you decide to return to work part-time. Most importantly it is vital to choose a pension that not only suits you today, but which offers you flexibility for life.

Protection

The word protection is often used to describe life and health insurance because that is exactly what these policies offer - they will protect your family's standard of living in the face of life's crises and will pay you a lump sum of money or a regular income to help you cope.

Life Assurance

While most people understand the need for life cover to enable them to pay off their mortgage if either partner dies, fewer people stop to consider how they are going to pay all of the bills on just one salary.

As a general rule of thumb, a married couple should

insure their lives for around ten times their combined annual salary, so that if one dies and the other is literally left 'holding the baby' the surviving partner has enough money left over to cope after repaying the mortgage. This is particularly true of women with young families where the cost of a child minder can often outweigh the benefit of going to work. Even where the woman has a low income - or no income at all - you should still be insured to help your partner cope with the children and bills if anything should happen to you.

Health Insurance

Whilst life assurance pays out if you die, there are various health insurance policies which will help you cope if you fall seriously ill, have an accident or become disabled. They fall into two main categories: those that pay a lump sum and those that replace most of your income until you retire if you are unable to ever work again. Lincoln say this is not as unlikely as you may think. At any one time there are over 1.5 million people registered as totally incapacitated by sickness or injury who have to rely on state benefits.

Critical Illness, Permanent Health Insurance and Accident, Sickness and Unemployment insurance are all valuable protection schemes which will keep your finances healthy even when you're not. Lincoln encourages all individuals, families, parents etc. to take out these types of insurance as they are the foundations of a happy lifestyle, and in the event that anything should happen you will still be able to manage.

Savings and Investment

Out of all the financial products which are available, savings products are one of the most easy to understand and most commonly taken out.

We're all familiar with the concept of saving, either in a bank or building society account, but fewer feel comfortable with shopping around for the best deal.

Whether you are saving on a regular basis or have a lump sum to make the most of, it always pays to look for the best rate with the minimum of hassle. The difference between instant access accounts can be as much as 5%. (3)

If you are willing to tie your money up for longer, then you can benefit from a higher rate of income and if you are prepared to take that little extra risk you may be rewarded even more.

With-profit, investment and guaranteed bonds are all ways of potentially beating building society returns whilst capping the amount of risk you are taking with your original capital investment.

Mortgages

At last, the UK's mortgage market has finally woken up to the needs of women and now offers a range of flexible mortgages to more appropriately reflect women's changing lifestyles.

Some mortgages now offer repayment 'holidays' to make it easier for periods where women stop working to have a family and the family is reduced to a single income for a short time. This makes it easier to budget at a time when there are additional costs of children to consider.

There are even one or two 'baby' mortgages now available which will allow you to borrow back some of the money you have repaid to help cover the costs of the new addition to the family.

More recently there are 'savings' mortgages which will allow you to overpay your mortgage on either a regular or lump sum basis. The pot of money you build up will earn the same rate of interest as you pay on your loan and the money can be accessed at any time in case of emergency.

Tax

Finally, all women, married and single, are now taxed as individuals and have their own tax allowance. At the moment, everyone can earn £4,045 a year without paying tax but when a couple marry they qualify for an additional married couple's allowance of £1,830 a year, this is still valuable even though it now only attracts tax relief at 15%. This is automatically added to the husband's allowance, although if you are working and your husband is not you may ask the tax man to transfer the allowance to you to lower the amount of tax you pay.

If money is the real key to independence then it is encouraging that women have more freedom than ever before. It now seems incredible that in the not too distant past, in some occupations, women who married were made to forfeit their jobs for the benefit of single women, because they had their husbands to provide for them!

In the 1990s, the decade which saw the introduction of the 'househusband', such a thing could simply not happen. In order to maintain their long-fought and hard-won individuality, women now need to safeguard, insure and protect their financial independence.

> Women have fought long and hard for political equality. Now it's time to seize control of your money matters too, says Louise Webber of Lincoln. Today, thankfully, you don't have to be a suffragette to prove your financial independence; simply taking out your own pension or opening a savings account will do!

The insurance industry has and is changing. It now recognises the need to address its audience on an individual basis, without the use of technical jargon. You can also be sure that all financial advisers are now trained to professional standards. So don't be put off.

Lincoln recommends that you find an adviser who is keen to provide you with the information that you need in order to make the choices you feel best address your priorities. Whether you choose an independent adviser or one from a company sales force, both are required to give 'best advice', only the finer details of the products may differ.

It is never too early or too late to improve your finances, so you can have the lifestyle you want and the ability to maintain it.

1) NOP Financial Marketing Pocket Book 1997

2) Pensions Pocket Book 1997 in
   conjunction with Bacon & Woodrow.

3) Moneyfacts

Lincoln is a marketing group regulated by the Personal Investment Authority providing life assurance, pensions and unit trusts.

13
Pensions and partners

Although it is imperative for women to build up their own independent pension, those who are in a marriage or partnership may want to do so in tandem with their partner's plans.

It is wise to take a close interest in your husband or partner's pension arrangements — not just in case you divorce, but also to identify any gaps in your joint planning. Is his pension large enough, for example, or is he relying on a contribution from you?

You should also find out what his company or private pension would pay to you and your children if he died before retirement, and fill any gaps in your life assurance as appropriate.

Those who are living together should check with scheme trustees whether it makes a difference that they are not actually married. If you are in a same-sex relationship, you should ask the scheme trustees about what would happen to your partner if you die. Some employers are sympathetic provided you inform them of a long-term relationship.

Pensions and divorce

What happens to pensions when a couple divorces is one of the biggest issues troubling the financial world at the moment. The husband's pension is often a couple's biggest asset after the family home.

But if you divorce, you have no automatic right to a share in it from your husband's company or private scheme, even if you did not get a chance to build up your own pension because you were caring for home and family and even if you helped to build it up for a self-employed partner.

If your husband remarries, his new wife will take over any pension benefits you had. The government is being lobbied at top level to change this unfair situation, but as yet, nothing has changed. This is a long recognised problem whose solution was still being considered at the time of writing.

Pensions must be negotiated as part of a divorce settlement. Valuing your husband's pension rights and your share is highly complex and outside the scope of most solicitors. Although it is expensive, it could be worth taking advice from a pensions specialist.

Recent pension changes include rules brought in by the Pensions Act 1995 mean that the value of your ex-spouse's pension should be taken into account when calculating the divorce settlement. It already has been for some years in Scotland.

But although this is an advance on the previous practice of ignoring the value of the man's pension rights, the way in which this is done is considered unsatisfactory both by women's lobbying groups and by pensions actuaries who have to calculate what sums are due to each of the splitting partners.

The way the English law currently works is that women receive a share of their former husband's pension when he retires through an attachment order on his future retirement payments. Many wanted the alternative options of receiving either a split of the pension pot, which would then be the divorced woman's own pension to which she could add, or a cash settlement which could be used to buy a personal pension if splitting was not possible.

The present 'attachment' system is unfair to women because:

- It ignores the 'clean break' principle at the heart of most divorce settlements.
- Young women may have to wait 30 to 40 years for a payment.
- They lose the attachment rights on remarriage.
- The husband might be able to delay taking a personal pen-

sion or structure a pension with a 'flexible' annuity so that only a small part of the pension becomes payable each year.

- There can be considerable disagreement over the exact valuation of the fund at the time of divorce which a clean split of the fund on a 50:50 or other agreed basis would avoid.
- The pension will be affected if the former husband dies — and there may be no widow's benefits or those benefits would go to a subsequent wife.
- The woman may miss out on growth — a wife of 20 years may well have contributed greatly to her ex-husband's success in the subsequent years of his working life.

The Pensions Industry wants a fairer way of sharing out pensions and, at the time of writing, the Government had published a consultative 'Green Paper' on Pension Rights on Divorce. But pensions concerns fear the cost of administering all the changes while the Government and the Treasury fear that some of the solutions proposed would cost extra tax relief.

There is unlikely to be further progress until at least 2000.

If you divorce and do not remarry before state pension age, you can qualify for a basic state pension based on your own and your ex-husband's National Insurance contributions. You can also claim a state pension on your ex-husband's record if you split up after state pension age.

More information

If you need financial advice, consult an adviser authorised by the Personal Investment Authority (PIA). Some advisers are independent, and can give guidance on all the products in the market-place. Others are tied to one company, and can only advise on its products. Make sure you know which type of adviser you are dealing with. It may be best to look for a 'fee-based' adviser who will buy in expertise from lawyers and accountants and then bill you. This may sound expensive — but it is worthwhile if it produces a more equitable share out of your ex's pension.

You can obtain specialist pensions advice from a member of:

The Society of Pension Consultants
St Bartholomew House
92 Fleet Street
London EC4Y 1DH
(postal enquiries only)

or:

The Association of Consulting Actuaries
1 Wardrobe Place
London EC4V 5AH
Tel: 0171-248 3163

Fair Shares is a pressure group campaigning for fair division of pensions on divorce:

Fair Shares
14 Park Road
Rugby
Warwickshire CV21 2QH

14
Living together

The number of couples living together has increased sharply in the past quarter of a century. A generation ago, in the early 1970s, just one in six women lived with their future husband before marriage. Now, according to official statistics, the proportion is two in three — and rising.

At the same time, the number of marriages has fallen by more than 10 per cent in the past ten years, because more couples are choosing to live together as a long-term alternative to marriage. The stigma of having a baby outside marriage is now fast disappearing. Nearly a third of all babies are born to unmarried mothers — of those, more than half are born to couples who live together and who choose to register the birth jointly.

But despite the increasing popularity of living together, both the law and the tax system give women who cohabit fewer rights than their married counterparts. Contrary to popular myth, you do not automatically gain rights similar to a married woman after you have lived with your boyfriend for a certain length of time. However, Social Security rules treat all couples in the same way whether they are married or co-habiting.

Common law marriage has not existed in England and Wales for more than 200 years, and in fact you have no automatic entitlement to a share in your partner's property or to widow's benefits, no matter how long you have been together or how many of his children you have had. The law in Scotland is different.

So if you are living with your partner, whether as a prelude to marriage or as a permanent arrangement, you need to be aware of the financial implications. Most of the potential problems can be avoided if you and your partner agree on what you want to happen financially if you split up or one of you dies, and then seeing a solicitor to draw up legal agreements and wills.

Your home

Moving in with a partner is a serious financial step. Women who are not married to their partner need to consider the following points very carefully:

- *Do you have any rights to the home?* If you move into a home your boyfriend owns in his sole name, you have no claim on it if your relationship breaks down. Whether you contributed towards the mortgage or expenses is irrelevant. The same applies if you move into rented accommodation that is in his name alone.

  But equally, if he moves into a home you are buying in your own name, he has no rights over it.

- *Who owns the property?* When you buy a home jointly with your partner, there are two different ways to own the property: joint tenancies and tenancies in common. If you are joint tenants and the other partner dies, their half of the house automatically passes to the other person. But if you are tenants in common, the deceased's share will go to their next of kin — which will not be their partner unless they specify so in a will. Tenants in common normally own a half share in the property, but ownership can be split in any other proportion, for instance 70 : 30 if one of you contributed much more to buying the property than the other.

- *Should we take out a joint endowment?* There's no need to. You can help make things easier if you do split up by each arranging a separate endowment or PEP in your own name to cover your half of the mortgage. Whether separate life cover is easily affordable compared with a joint life policy which pays out on just one death depends on your age, health and the amount of cover you require.

- *What happens if you split up?* If you want to remain in the home, your partner must agree to be taken off the mortgage deeds. You will then have to buy him out, and you will become responsible for the full mortgage.

You will need to seek permission from your bank or building society to have your partner's name taken off the deeds. They are entitled to refuse if they believe you will not be capable of meeting the mortgage instalments alone.

- *What happens if my partner absconds leaving me to pay the full mortgage?* Sadly, the most common cause of repossession is breakdown in relationships. When you take out a joint mortgage, both of you are jointly and severally liable for the full amount — so if your partner can't or won't pay, the lender can pursue you for the whole instalments.

  Keep your lender informed of any difficulties, and try to come to an arrangement where you carry on making payments of as much as you can afford. That way they are more likely to be sympathetic and less likely to repossess.

- *What is your tax position?* Unmarried couples can claim MIRAS — Mortgage Interest Relief at Source — on the interest on the first £30,000 of their home loan at 10 per cent. If you took out your mortgage before August 1988, you each receive MIRAS on £30,000, so you receive twice as much. But if you marry or take out a new mortgage, including a remortgage, you will only receive one tax relief. Few couples still benefit from double MIRAS.

Making a will

If your partner has not made a will, you will inherit *nothing* in England and Wales. The siuation can be different in Scotland. Everything he owns, including his share of your joint home, could go to his next of kin, whether that be children, parents, brothers and sisters — or even a separated wife to whom he is still legally married. If he has no next of kin, the government can claim the estate.

- Both partners should make a will to avoid such problems occurring. It is especially important to do so if you have children. A will also lets you appoint legal guardians for young children in case anything happens to you.

- A woman whose live-in partner dies without making a will can make a claim on some of his estate under the Inheritance (Provision for Family and Dependants) Act 1975. But this is complicated and expensive. Even if your claim is successful — which is far from guaranteed — it could be years before you see any money and your legal bills are likely to be high.

- Unmarried partners do not enjoy the same exemptions from inheritance tax as married women. Anything a husband or wife leaves to his or her spouse is free of inheritance tax. But if your unmarried partner leaves his estate to you, tax at 40 per cent is charged on anything over £215,000 (the nil rate band in the 1997/8 tax year). One way to avoid the tax is by taking out a life assurance policy. This is explained in more detail later in the chapter.

- If you marry later, you will both need to change your wills as the old ones become invalid.

Insurance

Life insurance should be a priority for anyone with dependants. Partners living together both need to take out an adequate amount of life cover, especially if you have children. Unmarried couples can take out a joint life assurance policy, which will pay out when the first partner dies. This is cheaper than taking out two single policies, but the surviving partner will no longer be insured after the policy has paid out, which is a problem if you are left with dependent children.

Taking out a joint policy can lead to problems when a couple splits up.

Alternatively, you can take out a single life policy written in trust for your partner. If you die, the money is paid direct to them, and is not classed as part of your estate. You can write a policy specifically intended to pay an expected inheritance tax bill if you wish. When both partners take out single life policies, the surviving partner will continue to be insured if the other dies, which is important if you have children.

Tax and benefits

The tax authorities treat unmarried couples as two single people. You both receive a single personal allowance (£4195 in the 1998/9 tax year). You will not get the Married Couples' Allowance, currently £1900.

Unmarried women with dependent children are entitled to the Additional Personal Allowance, also £1900. In the 1998/9 tax year, relief is granted at 15 per cent, so the cash value of the allowance is £285. You may also be able to claim against the child's father through the Child Support Agency.

Although you are treated as single people when it comes to receiving tax allowances, the DSS usually treats cohabitees as man and wife when you claim benefits. Both your incomes are taken into account when assessing your entitlement to means tested benefits such as Income Support and Housing Benefit. But for other contribution-based benefits, such as the Jobseekers Allowance, your partner's income is not taken into account.

Unmarried partners are not entitled to widow's benefits from the state.

Savings

You can set up joint savings accounts so the signature of both of you is needed to withdraw money, or so either one of you can sign. The same applies to bank accounts. Many unmarried couples keep separate accounts for individual use, and a joint one for bills. Both partners are equally liable for any debts run up on a joint account, regardless of which partner actually spent the money. You can specify that a joint account must not have an overdraft facility if you wish.

Pensions

It is unwise even for married women to rely on their husband's pension. Unmarried women should make even more effort to build up their own provision. Unlike married women, who may be able to claim up to half of their husband's company pension if he dies, you may have no entitlement. See Chapters 9 to 13 for more detail on pension planning.

More information

Independent financial advisers Fiona Price & Partners publish a factsheet, *Living Together*, available free from:

Fiona Price & Partners
33 Great Queen Street
Covent Garden
London WC2B 5AA
Tel: 0171-430 0366

The Child Poverty Action Group has authoritative books on both contributory and non-contributory state benefits and the Child Support Agency. Details from CPAG, 1–5 Bath Street, London EC1V 9PY.

The Consumers' Association publishes a helpful book, *Wills and Probate* and a *Make Your Will* action pack, available from the:

Consumers Association
2 Marylebone Road
London NW1 4DF
Tel: 0171-830 6000

FINANCES CRITICAL TO ILLNESS

Nearly three quarters (72%) of people do not believe that the state will care for them adequately if they are too ill to work, according to research undertaken for Midland Bank. Yet only six per cent have taken insurance cover to protect themselves and their families.

The chances of suffering from long term illness or disability are greater than you may imagine. Chilling Government statistics show that every year 600,000 people in the UK suffer a critical illness such as a heart attack, cancer or a stroke, and one in five working people will be off work through illness or accident for longer than three months. Many of them will never be able to return to their normal work again.

If you believe that it "won't happen to me" because you lead a healthy life and avoid hazards such as heavy smoking or dangerous sports, you may be underestimating the risks. The chances of being disabled for longer than six months before retirement is ten times greater than the risk of dying before retirement. In this situation, a life assurance policy may be of limited help and the pension may be a long way off.

The more generous employers pay employees while they're off work through illness – but even this is usually only for a specified time.

Many people make arrangements for their financial affairs to be dealt with if they die: such as repaying their mortgage, but Midland's research shows that few make provision for loss of earnings due to serious illness.

Household expenses take no account of your state of health. Indeed, it's worth considering that bills may increase if you spend more time at home or are incapacitated due to sickness. Some people are faced with having to use savings to pay for everyday essentials, or go without things they currently take for granted. If you become seriously ill, your financial commitments will not go away.

Fortunately however, a growing proportion are becoming more aware of the need to protect the quality of their lives from the financial problems posed by serious ill health. You can do this by taking out specially designed insurance cover.

There are two main options when considering cover in the event of a serious illness.

First, you can obtain insurance which will pay out a lump sum on the diagnosis of either a serious illness or a disability which is both permanent and total. This type of cover is available from a number of companies including Midland. The cover may extend for the whole of your life or it may be for a certain period only, such as the outstanding period left on your mortgage.

Secondly, you can obtain insurance which provides a replacement income to maintain your standard of living, should you suffer illness or disability. Cover can be extended to compensate for reduced earnings by providing a proportionate benefit if, as a result of your illness, you are forced to take a less-well paid job in the future. Again, Midland offers such cover.

It's important to arrange cover while you are well. An insurance policy will not cover you for conditions diagnosed before the insurance was arranged. Taking out cover in the event of serious illness removes the worry that the illness could also seriously damage your financial health.

**For further details, please contact your
local Midland Bank branch or call 0800 100166**

ADVERTISING COPY

15
Money and marriage

When you are in the throes of true love, it probably seems deeply unromantic to think about money. But no couple can escape the realities of having to deal with cash.

And whilst no one marries in the expectation they will get a divorce, it is possible to arrange your finances in such a way that the economic damage is minimised if you do split up. The most important thing for couples to do is to talk about money from the start.

Both should be aware of the other's debts and financial assets before marriage to avoid potential pitfalls and to maximise your joint finances. How much privacy and independence you want is obviously an individual issue, and each couple can come to their own arrangements. But it is always better that these are discussed fully and agreed on.

Money, lack of it and attitudes to it are major sources of rows between couples and can even be the cause of marital breakdown. If one of you is a spendthrift and the other is a skinflint, it is obviously going to be a problem area.

Couples should take an independent but complementary approach to joint financial planning. That way, you both have your own savings, pension and bank accounts under your sole control, which puts you in a better situation if things do go wrong. But it also allows you to plan in such a way that you can make the most of your joint assets.

Relying on your husband financially is nothing less than foolhardy. It leaves you extremely vulnerable in the event of a divorce or if you are widowed. Marriage will always entail giving up some financial independence. But the good news is that the bad old days when women had to get their husband's permission to take out a loan and were treated as his chattel in the eyes of the tax authorities are now over.

Preparing for the big day

Couples should start to think about financial planning well before they marry. The average cost of a wedding is now nearly £10,000 including a honeymoon, so unless you have very generous parents or want a minimum of fuss and show, you'll need to start saving well in advance.

You'll also have all the costs of setting up a new home and kitting it out. Beware of taking on too much credit at this stage — it's better to make do with second-hand furniture — call it a 'minimalist' approach — and wait until you've saved for what you want than ending up deep in debt.

Any marriage involves big financial changes. Young couples might be moving away from their parents' home and having to learn to budget for the first time.

But more established career women who delay marriage until their thirties may have built up fairly substantial assets in their own right and, for instance, have a flat to sell before moving into the marital home.

Pre-nuptial agreements laying down how a couple's property and assets would be split in the event of divorce are common in the United States. They strike most British people as distasteful, however, and in any case are not binding in English law. If you have substantial wealth in your own right it may be worth transferring it into a trust fund. This requires expert advice.

Tax and marriage

The tax advantages of marriage are not as great as they once were, but wedding bells do still bring some tax perks:

● Since 1990, women have been treated as independent people in the eyes of the tax authorities, instead of just a chattel of their husband. It means you will enjoy privacy over your tax affairs — but the downside is you are responsible for filling in your own tax return.

- Husband and wife are each taxed on their own income and capital gains, and each have their own tax-free Personal Allowance, £4195 in the 1998/9 tax year.
- When you marry you become entitled to the Married Couples' Allowance of £1990 in the 1998/9 tax year. Relief on the allowance is granted at 15 per cent in 1998/9, so its value is just £285. It will fall to 10 per cent — £190 in cash terms — in 1999/2000.
- The allowance automatically goes to the husband. But the wife can claim half without his permission. If both partners agree, the wife can have the full allowance, provided you tell the tax authorities before the end of the previous tax year.
- In the year of marriage, the allowance is reduced by 1/12 for each month after the end of the tax year in April in which you are still single. So if you marry on 14 May, you will receive 11/12 of the allowance.
- The tax authorities allow relatives to give you cash wedding presents free of inheritance tax. Each parent of the bride or groom can give up to £5000 tax free, grandparents can give £2500 and anyone else can give you £1000.

Joint savings and investments

It makes sense for married couples to have savings and investments in their own name, not just to give them independence, but to make the most of tax breaks:

- Husband and wife each have their own tax-free allowance for Personal Equity Plans, TESSAs, National Savings and the new Individual Savings Accounts. It makes sense for you both to make use of the tax shelters.
- Any profits you make on shares or other assets are subject to capital gains tax. But husbands and wives each have their own annual tax-free allowance, £6800 in the 1998/9 tax year. So if one of you will exceed the tax-free threshold, you can save tax by transferring assets to your partner. Gifts of assets between man and wife are free of capital gains tax or inheritance tax — but gifts to anyone else may incur a tax charge.

● If one partner earns less than the other and pays tax at a lower rate, it makes sense to transfer investments into their name. That way, the interest or dividends will be taxed at a lower rate. But any gifts of this sort must be outright, with no strings attached.

Making a will

Any will you made while you were still single becomes invalid when you marry, so you will need to make a new one. If you or your husband have not yet made a will, you must both do so as soon as possible.

Clearly, this is a sensitive subject, and many people irrationally feel the very thought of making a will is 'tempting fate'. But if your husband does not make a proper will, you will be left in a very vulnerable situation.

Wives do not automatically inherit everything when their husband dies, in spite of persistent myths to that effect.

If there is no will — known as dying intestate — and you have children, the widow gets the first £125,000 of the estate, and a life interest in half the rest. A life interest means you can draw interest or use possessions, but you cannot sell anything or draw on capital. The other remaining half goes to the children, who also inherit the capital bearing the life interest when the widow dies.

If there are no children, the widow gets the first £200,000 of the estate, and half the remainder. The remaining half is shared between other relatives.

This may sound like a lot of money and not relevant to you. But many people underestimate the value of their estate, especially when you add in the family home. The rules for 'intestacy' are different in Scotland. The amounts can also change with time as they are intended to reflect the will of an 'average' person.

Making a tax-efficient will can also help minimise or avoid inheritance tax, which is payable on estates worth more than £223,000. You can draw up a will so that husband and wife both make use of their own £223,000 allowance.

Life cover is a must

Both of you should have adequate life cover, to make sure the other will not be thrown into financial hardship if anything happens. State benefits for widows are not generous — the widowed mother's allowance, for instance, most likely to be claimed by younger women with children, is paid at a full rate of £64.70 in 1998/9.

Young fathers suddenly left with children to support are even worse off — there are no state benefits especially for widowers.

More information

The Inland Revenue publishes some useful leaflets, available in tax offices: IR80, *Income Tax and Married Couples*, and IR110, *A Guide for People with Savings*.

We heard you wanted...

an easy, inexpensive way to cover yourself against serious illness.

Midland

The Listening Bank

Call 0800 100 166

Every year thousands of people are struck by illnesses that leave them permanently unable to work. Protecting our families against this is something we all must consider.

That's why Midland, the U.K's leading provider of critical illness cover, has put together a pack that explains how quick, easy and inexpensive it can be to protect your income against serious health problems.

'Source: LIMRA, May 1997.

Call for details

or visit a branch

or cut the coupon.

For your free protection pack, complete and return the coupon to:
Midland Bank plc, Family Protection, FREEPOST SWB 332, Bristol, BS1 6BR.

Mr/Ms/Mrs/Miss/Other (please specify)	Initials	Surname
House name/number	Street	
Town		
County	Postcode	
Daytime tel no (inc. STD)	Evening tel no (inc. STD)	SI31

Do you hold other Midland accounts? ☐ Yes ☐ No (please tick). If so please fill in your sort code 4 0 ☐☐ ☐☐☐

May we send you information about our products and services in future? ☐ Yes ☐ No (please tick).

16
Financial family planning

Few couples appreciate the true price of parenthood before their children arrive. It may be just as well, for according to a survey by *Moneywise* magazine, the total cost of bringing up a child for the first 16 years could come to a massive £250,000 in a traditional family where the mother gives up work and stays at home until the child is a teenager. That doesn't include expensive 'extras' such as a nanny, private school fees or higher education. This amount is largely nonsensical. It equates to an after tax income of around £15,000 per child each year. Very few families could afford both this and food! But children are expensive nevertheless.

It is advantageous to plan financially, if you can, preferably before your baby is even conceived!

First steps

When your baby is born you will need to budget for clothes, prams and equipment, and perhaps much larger expenses if you want to move to a bigger house, say, or extend your present home. If you decide to take a break from work, you may also want to build up your own independent savings. So even if you don't have any immediate plans to start a family, it is worth saving for the future.

If you have five or more years to go before you plan to have children, you have time to save a tidy sum. Tax-free options include a TESSA, where you can save up to £9000 over five years, National Savings certificates and Individual Savings Accounts (from April 1999). Some building societies and banks offer better rates to regular savers. See Chapters 2 and 3 for more details.

Women who want to have children in the future should also try to pay extra into their pension plan while they can to make up for the time they will lose whilst bringing up a family. See Chapter 11 for more information.

Of course, most young couples do not map out their lives so far ahead, and often cannot afford to set aside large sums while they are also meeting the costs of setting up a first home. But it is still possible to do some forward planning.

Many prospective parents want to move to a larger home before they start a family. It may be sensible to take out a fixed rate mortgage covering the first two to five years, so that you are sure what your repayments will be and you are protected from interest rate rises. There is no guarantee that these will be cheaper than variable rate loans. After all, they are funded by big financial institutions who believe they can make money by betting against the fixed rate. But they do provide security against an increase. Think of any extra you pay as 'insurance'.

Protecting your family

Life insurance is an absolute necessity for couples intending to have children. You will need higher cover in the early years, and less when the children are grown up and no longer dependent on you. Wives — or husbands — who stay at home to care for the kids still need insurance. You can structure life insurance either to pay a lump sum or an annual income for a fixed number of years.

A more recent option is 'critical illness' cover. This promises a payment if the policyholder suffers one of a number of serious illnesses such as cancer or a heart-attack.

Better off parents may be able to afford Permanent Health Insurance (PHI). Policyholders can claim a regular income if they are unable to work up to their retirement age. PHI cover can be bought for non-earning spouses. Policies for women usually cost 50 per cent more than similar plans for men. This 'loading' is controversial.

All parents should make a will. If you do not, your family can be left in financial chaos, and your money might not go to the people you wished. A will also allows you to name a guardian for your child in case anything happens to you.

Benefits for mothers

Child Benefit is paid to all mothers at £11.45 per week in 1998/9 for the first child and £9.30 a week for each other child under 16 (or under 19 if they are still in full-time education). Single parents can also claim One Parent Benefit, paid at a single rate of £6.30 per week regardless of how many children you have but this is being phased out from 1998.

In addition, pregnant women are entitled to free maternity care, free dental care, free parenthood preparation classes and free prescriptions. After the birth you are entitled to free dental care and prescriptions for up to one year. If you have a low income, you can continue to claim free healthcare on a means-tested basis.

School fees

Proud parents who are ambitious to send their children to Eton or Cheltenham Ladies College — or even a modest private school — need to plan particularly carefully. It is not just the wealthy who want to give their children the advantage of a private education. But sending your child to a day school can cost between £3000 and £8000 a year, rising to £6000 to £12,000 for boarders.

Your options for school fees planning depend on your timescale, your tax position, and how much risk you are prepared to take.

The basic ways of paying are:

- Pay the fees as you go out of your income.
- Take out a loan or second mortgage to pay.
- Invest a lump sum or make regular savings in advance.

Option three is the ideal one — it will make the whole process less painful, and appear to cost you less each year.

If you have more than five years to plan ahead for school fees, your investment choices include educational trusts, endowment policies or tax-free share plans such as PEPs or Individual Savings Accounts.

In the medium term, if you have five years or less to go, consider tax-free TESSAs, savings accounts, including long-term fixed rates and deposit accounts. But there are no magic solutions. One way or another you pay heavily for the privilege of privilege — whatever so-called 'school fees' advisers pretend.

Saving for children

Parents and grandparents are often keen to give their children a good start in life by setting up savings accounts for them. Provided your child's income does not exceed his or her personal allowance, any savings income is tax-free. Make sure you register your child as a non-taxpayer using form R85, available from banks and building societies, so he or she will receive her savings interest with no tax deducted.

But there are controls on the amount of money parents can put into savings accounts in a child's name, designed to avoid tax evasion. If more than £100 is earned on money that came from either parent in any one tax year, it will be taxed. Each parent has their own £100 limit, so the child can earn up to £200 if mum and dad both make gifts. At a 5 per cent building society interest rate, this gives a maximum £4000 capital sum. 'Tax free' investments such as National Savings or Friendly Society plans do not count towards this total.

If the money comes from grandparents, however, the clause does not apply. Grandparents can also cut down potential inheritance tax bills by making gifts to children during their lifetimes. They can give a total of up to £3000 each tax year free of tax, along with an unlimited number of gifts up to £250.

National Savings Children's Bonus Bonds are a good home for up to £1000 of savings – the interest is tax-free. Accounts are designed to run for five years.

If you can commit yourself to saving on behalf of a child or grandchild for ten years, a friendly society Baby Bond could be an option, provided you are sure you can afford to keep up the payments. The maximum investment is £25 per month or £270 a year, and many schemes offer 'half plans'. The bonds are linked to the stock market and the payout is tax-free. But if you cash in before ten years, you may get nothing or very little back. See Chapters 2 and 3 for more detail.

More information

The Independent Schools Information Service publishes a guide to independent schools and a range of booklets covering ways to fund school fees and information on scholarships and grants:

ISIS
56 Buckingham Gate
London SW1E 6AG
Tel: 0171-630 8793

Take control of your family finances

ABC Bonus Account

The easy way to *control* your household *budget*

With so many different bills to pay, keeping a grip on the business of running your family's outgoings can be trying, especially when everything comes out of just one bank account! In an ideal world we would all like to be able to budget and plan ahead by keeping tabs on our transactions and by keeping household finances separate from other spending money.

That is why Abbey National has teamed up with Safeway to offer you a new type of household account, the ABC Bonus Account.

It gives you convenience and control by letting you arrange for expenses like gas, electricity, credit card and council tax bills to all come out of just one dedicated household account as well as using the account to pay for your weekly food, shopping and petrol.

SAFEWAY

ABBEY NATIONAL

Safeway Stores PLC Registered Office: 6 Millington Road, Hayes, Middlesex UB3 4AY, UK.
Abbey National PLC Registered Office: Abbey House, Baker Street, London NW1 6XL, UK.

As easy as 'ABC'

● The ABC Bonus Account card is a combined cashpoint and payment card.

● Use it to pay for your shopping at over 400 Safeway stores.

● It is accepted at over 160,000 outlets nationwide displaying the Electron sign.

● Use your card to withdraw up to £250* per day from any Abbeylink, Link or PLUS cash machine worldwide.

● Receive Cashback from a Safeway cashier of up to £100 when you use your card to pay for shopping.

● Paying your other bills is easy either by setting up direct debits, standing orders or using the dedicated bill payment service which allows you to control the amount that goes out of your account and also when it goes out, either by using the Telephone Banking Service or any Abbeylink cash machine.

● Purchases on your card are debited from your Account balance instantly so you always know exactly how much is left.

● You can always phone up and check your balance 24-hours a day using the Telephone Banking Service.

This new account offers convenience, control, saves you time and gives you the added benefit of an attractive interest rate on your balance.

Simply add up your household outgoings nd arrange a standing order from your main ank account into your ABC Bonus Account minimum £50).

hen all your household expenses will be onveniently under one roof.

When you open your ABC Account, you ill be rewarded with valuable ABC points hen you shop at Safeway.

These points can be redeemed for free roducts, savings or family offers, and as well s earning 1 point for every £1 spent, you'll so receive 500 extra points when you open n account.

What's more, for 12 weeks after you first se your card at Safeway to pay for your hopping you will earn EXTRA points.△

ABC Bonus Account is available to nyone aged over 18, subject only to name nd address confirmation, opening an ccount could not be easier.

Simply visit your local Safeway store and ck up a leaflet, or alternatively call 0800)5 995* and ask for an application pack

Call freephone on
0800 995 995*

*There will be a charge for cash withdrawals from non-Abbeylink machines. A tariff of charges will be provided with your application pack.
△Promotional details correct at time of going to press.
*To assist us in improving our service we may record or monitor telephone calls.

17
Your maternity rights

The decision to have a baby brings many new considerations for working women. Whether you want to return to work full or part time, work at home or devote yourself to motherhood depends on individual preference and on what you can afford.

But it makes sense to know your rights at work, and to discuss the alternatives — and their financial consequences — fully with your partner or family.

Maternity rights for working women

New rules came into effect during 1994 giving pregnant women improved legal rights at work, along with new maternity benefit rules. Some of the most important aspects of the new rules, which apply to women in England, Scotland and Wales are described below. The position in Northern Ireland is similar but not exactly the same.

While you are pregnant

- Whether you work full or part time, you are entitled to reasonable time off for ante-natal care, with pay. This can include not only medical examinations but also relaxation and parentcraft classes.
- It is against the law for an employer to dismiss a woman or select her for redundancy purely or mainly because she is pregnant or has given birth.
- If you are dismissed during pregnancy or maternity leave you are entitled to a written statement of the reasons.

Time off to have a baby

- All pregnant employees are entitled to at least fourteen weeks statutory maternity leave, regardless of their length of service or hours of work.
- During that period, you are entitled to all the benefits of your contract, such as holiday rights and payments by your employer into a company pension scheme. You are not automatically entitled to receive pay, though you may qualify for Statutory Maternity Pay.
- If you have worked for the same employer full time (at least 16 hours a week) for at least two continuous years, you are also entitled to an additional period of maternity absence on top of your maternity leave.
- Maternity absence lasts from the end of your maternity leave until the 28th week after your baby is born. Part-timers must have worked at least 8 hours a week for five continuous years to qualify for maternity absence. The period of continuous employment is calculated up to the eleventh week before your baby is due. Your employer must keep your job open for you if you wish to return.

Maternity benefits

There are two main benefits pregnant women can claim: Statutory Maternity Pay and Maternity Allowance.

- Your employer must pay SMP if you have worked for them continuously for 26 weeks up to and including the fifteenth week before you expect your baby to be born. Your average earnings for the eight weeks up to and including the fifteenth week before the expected birth must have been at least £64 a week.
- If you fulfil those conditions, you are entitled to at least 18 weeks' SMP, whether or not you intend to return to work. SMP is only payable while you are absent from work, but you can carry on working right up until the birth and still keep your 18 week entitlement.

- For the first six weeks you will receive SMP at 90 per cent of your average weekly earnings, with a minimum payment of £57.50. It is paid in the same way and at the same time as your normal earnings. During the remaining 12 weeks, you will receive a flat SMP payment of £57.50. All the rates quoted apply to 1998/9. SMP is taken into consideration for Income tax and National Insurance. But if that is all you receive you must claim National Insurance credits.
- If you are not entitled to SMP, your employer must fill in DSS form SMP1, and give it to you, to help you claim Maternity Allowance.
- Women who do not qualify for SMP but have paid National Insurance contributions in 26 out of the 66 weeks ending with the week before they expect their baby to arrive are entitled to claim a maximum of 18 weeks' Maternity Allowance if:
  - either they are employed but do not qualify for SMP; or
  - they have recently been employed; or
  - they are self-employed.
- You can claim on form MA1, available from Benefits Agencies or ante-natal clinics. Maternity Allowance is only payable when you are not at work. It is usually paid by order book, which can be cashed each week at a post office of your choice.
- You receive a sum of £57.50 a week if you were employed during the fifteenth week before your baby is due, or £50.10 if you were not employed or you were self-employed. These rates are for 1998/9. There are additions for adult dependants.
- If you are not entitled to SMP or Maternity Allowance, you may still be able to claim Income Support. For more information, see DSS leaflet IS1, *Income Support*. Women who qualify for Income Support may be able to claim up to £100 from the Social Fund on the birth of a child.

What you must tell your employer — and when

If you want to claim maternity leave and SMP, you must tell your employer you are pregnant, and when you expect the baby to be born. Normally, you will need a medical certificate as confirmation. If you want to go back to work after a period of maternity absence, you should mention this at the same time.

You should also tell your employer when you intend to start your maternity leave and when you want to receive SMP. You must make both these notifications at least 21 days before you intend to start taking maternity leave.

If you want to go back to work immediately after the end of your maternity leave, you do not have to give advance notice to your employer.

But if you want to return before then, you should give your employer seven days' notice of your date of return. Women who take maternity absence as well (see above) must give 21 days notice of their date of return. Your employer may send you a written request to confirm you intend to return to work. The earliest they can write is 21 days before the end of your maternity leave. If you do not reply within 14 days, you lose the right to return.

More information:

Employment Rights for Expectant Mothers and *Maternity Benefits: A Guide for Employers and Employees* are free booklets, both available from Job Centres.

The Department of Social Security also has two useful publications: NI 17A, *A Guide to Maternity Benefits*, and FB8, *Babies and Benefit*, available from Benefits Agencies, some post offices and public libraries.

The Child Poverty Action Group publishes *Rights Guide to Non Means-Tested Benefits* (£8.95) from CPAG, 1–5 Bath Street, London EC1V 9PY.

18
Widowhood

Women are five times more likely to attend the funeral of their partner than men. It is a simple demographic fact based on women living longer and tending to marry when younger than their partners. No amount of financial planning can bring back a deceased loved one. But cash can help make daily life more bearable — especially if you have children or have retired.

You do not need any legal forms to gain access to bank and other accounts held in your joint names. You should, however, inform the bank or building society of the death. But you must go through Probate — a legal procedure — before you can claim on an account in your husband's name that has been left to you in his will. If he died without a will — intestate— his estate will be divided up in a pre-ordained manner. This mainly affects women whose husbands have substantial assets.

Most occupational pension schemes provide an income for a widow and any dependent children. This should be paid whether your husband had retired or not. If he was still working, you may qualify for a lump sum of up to four times his salary from his company scheme.

Many personal pension plans have built-in life cover. But in any case, you should get a return of contributions plus any investment growth or interest. A few old schemes merely give back the payments your late husband made without any growth even if they were paid over many years ago.

If your husband had bought all the life and other forms of cover that the insurance industry sells, you will be financially assured. But few can afford to buy all the myriad protection policies. A family on average earnings would have little left to feed and clothe themselves if they purchased all the products sold 'to give peace of mind'.

The reality is that you are likely to be left with a small amount from an insurance company and the rest of your life. What should you do with any of this cash lump sum that is left over after you pay the bills?

If you are elderly, you could put a sum into an annuity — a device which gives you a guaranteed income every month for the rest of your life although you will have sacrificed the capital. It is a sort of life assurance in reverse. Instead of paying in each month and receiving a lump sum when you die, you receive a monthly payout and lose your lump sum. Annuities are not just complicated — there are huge differences between the rates on offer from companies. Always take independent financial advice.

Houseowning women with no children — or those that do not wish to hand on their estate to their family through their will — can opt for one of the 'home income plans' which turns the value of their property into a regular income in return for losing part or all of it when they die. The Bank of Scotland and Barclays Bank have a zero per cent mortgage deal which gives much the same result.

Again, no one should enter a home income plan without taking both independent financial advice and seeking help from a solicitor. You should also talk this move over with your family if you have any. Reputable home income plan concerns insist on independent financial and legal advice and a discussion with your children as a matter of course.

Both the above courses best apply to those aged at least 75. If you are younger, you should consider either a high interest rate building society plan if you want to guarantee your original capital, a corporate bond personal equity plan for high income with some risk or, if you do not mind day-to-day fluctuations in your capital, an income producing unit trust.

If you are still working — perhaps you are in your fifties and your children if any have moved out and you do not need immediate income — you should aim for a unit trust which combines a growing income with a good chance of increasing your capital.

But the fact is that only a minority of widows receive more than the proverbial mite. Older women and younger women with children are likely to end up dependent, at least in part, on the state.

Social security for widows

Social security payments divide into those you get by right if you or your former spouse paid the correct number of National Insurance contributions and those that are means-tested.

Contributory benefits

To claim as a widow in England and Wales, you must have been legally married at the time of his death. In Scotland, both legal marriage and the common law formula of 'by cohabitation with habit and repute' are recognised. If you were divorcing your husband at the time of death, you are entitled to benefits as long as the decree was not absolute — even if you are, as you probably will be, living apart from him.

There is a death grant of £1000 paid of right if your late husband fulfilled certain National Insurance conditions or died of a recognised industrial disease *and* you were either under 60 when he died or if you were over 60, he had not yet begun to draw his state retirement pension.

A 'widowed mother's allowance' is paid if you are either pregnant and/or have a child who qualifies for child benefit. This is payable at £64.70 a week (in 1998/9 and rising in line with prices in subsequent years in common with most other weekly paid benefits) plus an amount for each qualifying child.

This allowance stops once all your children have either passed the age of 19 or stopped full-time education after which you may qualify for the widow's pension. The Widowed Mother's Allowance ceases on remarriage and is suspended if you are cohabiting.

The widow's pension is paid at £64.70 a week — the same as the standard old age pension — if you were at least 55 when he died and he had a good contributions record. If you were younger when he died, there is a sliding scale down to the age of 45. You will be entitled to the £10 Christmas Bonus — a sum unchanged since it was first introduced over a quarter of a century ago. It would now have to be at least £100 to keep up with inflation.

Means-tested payments

Widows and other women whose income is below a threshold considered correct for their needs including housing and the care of dependent children — this is called the Applicable Amount — should apply to the Department of Social Security for Income Support, Family Credit or other means-tested benefits. Post offices have a simple form you can fill in to request a visit from a DSS officer. You are unlikely to need to visit the local DSS office.

More information

The Child Poverty Action Group publishes guides to both *National Welfare Benefits* (means-tested) and *Non-Means Tested Benefits* at £8.95 each (reduced prices for claimants). Details from CPAG, 1–5 Bath Street, London EC1V 9PY, tel: 0171-253 3406.

19
Combining work and home

More and more women return to work after having a baby, either to fulfil their career ambitions or simply to make ends meet. But for most the decision is not an easy one. You and your husband or partner need to work out the most suitable solution in terms of hours and working arrangements. But whatever you decide, there will be repercussions for your finances.

It is worth carrying out a basic cost/benefit analysis to help work out the financial consequences of your decision. On the benefit side are the wages or salary you will earn. On the cost side you need to list the expenses of childcare.

The government has introduced measures to help lower income families with children get back into the workforce. People on Family Credit and Housing Benefit can deduct up to £60 a week from their income calculation towards the cost of a registered childminder, day nursery or other arrangement to care for a child or children under the age of 11. Childcare is not normally tax-deductible. However if your employer provides a creche as a non-cash benefit, the value will not be taxed providing the employer is involved with the management. If you receive cash or vouchers for childcare, you will face an income tax bill.

Even so, after knocking off the expense of a childminder or nanny, it may not look worthwhile returning to work purely on financial grounds. But you also need to think about the 'sanity factor' — whether you need to get out of the house — and the longer-term implications. If you carry on working you may be able to command salary increases or promotions in future, whereas if you take a break until your children are older, you may have to return to work at a lower level.

Find out what your employer offers. If you return to work immediately after your statutory maternity leave or absence, you are entitled to come back to the same job, with the same terms and conditions. But some companies allow you to take longer breaks of several years after which you can return to a job of equal status. Usually you will be expected to do several weeks' work a year to keep in touch.

Part-time work

Many women opt to return to work part time after the birth of a baby, or seek out flexible working arrangements.

About one in four of all employees in Britain is a part-timer, and more than four out of five of these are women.

For the purposes of employment rights, part time means working between eight and 16 hours a week. Under the 'hours rule' part-timers doing less than 16 hours a week traditionally had to work for five years to win the right to bring an unfair dismissal claim or receive statutory redundancy pay, whilst full-timers only need two years' service.

They were also often excluded from company pension schemes. A recent case in the House of Lords decided that the 'hours rule' was discriminatory and part-timers should have the same rights as full-timers after two years' service.

Part-timers should not be denied membership to the company pension scheme simply because of the fact they work fewer hours.

Many part-timers get pro-rata holidays, sometimes including bank holidays. Whether or not you receive other benefits such as staff discounts, cheap mortgages or season ticket loans varies from company to company.

Flexible working

In addition to straightforward part-time work, your employer may offer you flexible working options such as job-sharing, flexitime and term-time working.

Job-sharing is where you share one full-time job with another worker. This is often a sensible solution — but you need a good relationship with your co-worker for it to succeed. If your employer operates a flexitime scheme, you can choose the times at which you start and stop work, within limits.

Some employers also operate annual hours schemes, where you contract to work a certain number of hours each year, but have some flexibility over when you do them.

If your employer does not have any formal schemes for flexible working, you may be able to negotiate a deal.

Working from home

Modern technology means many jobs can now be done from home with the aid of a telephone and a computer terminal. It can allow women to tailor their work to the needs of their family, and means big savings in both time and money on travel. But you will still need to make childcare arrangements if you have children under school age.

Some companies, including BT and computer giant ICL, allow selected employees to work from home. Alternatively, you may join the ranks of self-employed people who run a business from home. But beware of exploitative schemes. A report by the National Group on Homeworking found up to a million homeworkers, mainly women, earned an average of £1.28 an hour, with some working for as little as 30p an hour.

If you are self-employed and working at home, there are a number of financial factors to consider:

- You may be eligible for tax relief on a proportion of your heating, lighting, cleaning and insurance bills.
- If you use part of your home solely for business, you may be liable for capital gains tax on any profits you make on that part if you sell your home.
- If you use part of your home for business purposes without telling your insurance company, it could invalidate your

home insurance policy especially if customers visit you or
you keep goods on your premises.

More information

The Women Returners' Network aims to help women get back
to work or gain new qualifications:
The Women Returners' Network
8 John Adam Street
London WC2N 6EZ
Tel: 0171-468 2290

Parents at Work is a charity providing information on childcare
and on companies operating family-friendly policies.

Parents at Work
45 Beach Street
London EC2Y 8AD
Tel: 0171-588 0802

Educational charity New Ways to Work provides free advice and
information for people who would like to work flexibly.

New Ways to Work
309 Upper Street
London N1 2TY
Tel: 0171-226 4026

The Consumers' Association publishes an excellent book, the
Which? Guide to Earning Money At Home, available from the
Which? Bookshop, 359–61 Euston Road, London NW1, or tel:
0800 252100. *Teach Yourself Women's Studies* has information
on employment matters from a feminist perspective.

20

Women mean business

A quarter of self-employed people are women, an increase of nearly two-thirds on ten years ago. And almost one third of new business start-ups are now run by female entrepreneurs.

Although most women will not end up running a multi-million pound international empire like Anita Roddick's original small business which ended up as the Body Shop, research shows their businesses may have a better chance of success because they are more inclined than men to seek training.

Self-employment can offer women with families more flexibility over when they work. But since the average self-employed person works 75 hours a week, it doesn't mean you will have more time to spend with family and friends.

Your business plan

All would-be business women should draw up a business plan as a first step. This is essential for when you approach your bank or another backer for finance, and will also help clarify all aspects of the idea in your own mind. Don't just view the business plan as a number-crunching exercise to keep the bank manager happy. It should cover all aspects of the business and you should review it at regular intervals after starting up to see how far you are achieving your aims. It should include:

- A brief description of your business.
- Details of your target market, your main competitors, and why you think you can succeed.
- What the unique selling point is of the business.
- Your CV, detailing your past experience and qualifications, stressing those relevant to the new business. If you have a business partner, include their CV as well.

- Details of how you intend to price your product or service, and how you have arrived at the figure.
- How you see the business developing in the future.
- A cash flow forecast, showing the money you expect to come in and go out and a profit forecast. Detail how you arrive at the figures. This will show how likely the proposition is to succeed. Banks will normally provide you with forms for this.
- The amount of capital you are putting into the business.
- The amount of money you need to raise in addition to get the business off the ground, and details of any security you can offer, eg your home, and how you intend to repay.
- Details of any other sources of finance, eg loans from family.

Banks are the main source of finance for small businesses. If you take out a business loan, you are normally expected to offer security, for instance your home or a life assurance policy. If you are a married woman, your bank may ask your husband to guarantee the loan. If you are using a jointly owned home as security for a business loan, your husband should get independent financial advice before signing any guarantees. You may also be eligible for loans and grants.

Tax, VAT and financial planning

You must inform the Inland Revenue that you have started up a business, and fill in form 41G. Also tell the Department of Social Security and fill in form CF11 giving details of your business and your National Insurance number. It's worth employing an accountant to help with your tax affairs. Self-employed people pay tax on the profit they have made, less various business expenses including accountancy.

If your profits after expenses are more than £3590 in the 1998/9 tax year, you have to pay Class 2 National Insurance contributions at a rate of £6.35 a week. And if your profits are more than £7310, you must pay Class 4 National Insurance contributions at 6 per cent of your profit over £6860 up to £25,220. Class

4 contributions are effectively a tax. They give no benefits. DSS leaflet FB30, *Self-Employed? A Guide to Your NI Contributions and Social Security Benefits*, gives more information.

If the turnover of your business is more than £50,000 in the 1998/9 tax year, you must also register for VAT. You can opt to do so if you have a lower turnover — in some cases this can be advantageous. VAT leaflet VAT700/1, *Should I be registered for VAT?* gives more information. Remember, this applies to your sales and not your profits.

Women starting their own business also need to take care of some other important aspects of financial planning. You should have life cover to take care of any business debts in case anything happens to you. A pension plan is a priority, and also consider permanent health insurance in case you fall ill for a long period. But don't expect a bargain. PHI rates are around 50 per cent higher for women than for men.

More information

Inland Revenue leaflets IR 28, *Starting in Business*, IR 57, *Thinking of Working for Yourself*, IR 104, *Simple Tax Accounts*, and IR 105, *How your Profits are Taxed*, are all useful.

The *Lloyds Bank Small Business Guide* by Sara Williams is an invaluable handbook. It is published by Penguin and is available in bookshops price £15.00.

The Women's Enterprise Forum aims to help female entrepreneurs. Write to:

The Women's Enterprise Forum
c/o Sandra Brusby
Warrington Business Venture
Warrington Business Park
Chadwick House
Warrington Road
Risley
Warrington WA3 6AE
Tel: 01925 668040

NatWest Bank has produced a publication, *The Business Start-up Guide,* including specimen business plans, cashflow and profit forecasts, available free from any branch. The bank also produces a *Small Business Information Directory* which details the help available locally to small businesses, such as local grants, support groups and export initiatives. It is free and locally tailored by postcode.

The BDO Stoy Hayward *Guide to the Family Business* (Kogan Page £12.95) is excellent on the dynamics and difficulties of the family firm.

21
Dealing with divorce

All too many women are forced to deal with the financial consequences of divorce and of being a single parent.

Divorce is at historically high levels. For every hundred marriages in the early 1990s, there are now 58 divorces. It seems to be a popular male belief that women use divorce as an excuse to take their ex-husband to the cleaners. But the truth is women are far more likely to suffer financially as a consequence of marital breakdown, especially if they are left with young children. Nine out of ten lone parents, of whom more than half are divorced women, are dependent on state benefits to survive.

If you have just decided to divorce or separate, it is an emotionally traumatic time. Often, money can become yet another battleground for a sparring couple, and negotiating a fair financial settlement can be extremely stressful. For some women, who have always left the family finances to their husband, there is the additional stress of having to make money decisions for the first time.

A financial settlement

Your basic aim is to negotiate a fair financial settlement for yourself and your children. At this stage, your husband's solicitor may ask you for a statement of your income and outgoings. It makes sense to take stock in any case, so you can realistically appraise the situation, and perhaps identify any ways of improving it, such as cutting down on expenses.

You will be entitled to a proportion, not necessarily half, of your joint assets. The most important of these, in most cases, are the family home and the man's pension rights.

There are no hard and fast rules over what share of the assets you should have, or on the level of maintenance for yourself, though maintenance for your children is covered by the Child Support Act.

Find a good solicitor who specialises in divorce to help you. Remember you may be entitled to Legal Aid — leaflets are available from your solicitor or your local Citizen's Advice Bureau, or from the Legal Aid Board.

You do not have to accept the first offer your ex-spouse makes. But try to be realistic. And remember that the bad behaviour of either partner is very rarely taken into account when deciding on financial settlements. Apart from highly exceptional cases, a court would consider it irrelevant.

Amicable agreements normally keep legal costs down. Around 3500 solicitors are members of the Solicitors' Family Law Association, which aims to help parting couples settle as cheaply and painlessly as possible.

The family home

There are various options you could take over the family home:

- Sell the home and divide the proceeds between you. This is unlikely to be a good option if you have children, because unless you have enough capital to buy a new home adequate for your family needs, you may be forced into one that is too small. Indeed, you may not be left with enough to buy a new home at all.
- Postpone the sale of the home until your children are no longer dependent. Under this arrangement, you stay in the family home, which is sold when your kids grow up. At that stage, the proceeds are divided between you and your former husband. This arrangement is often suggested by solicitors. But it may cause you problems in the future if you don't have enough money then to buy out your ex-spouse's share or to buy a new home.
- Buy out your ex-husband's share now. If you can afford to do this, it may well be the best option, because it provides

stability for you and your children. Talk to your lender about having your ex-husband's name taken off the deeds, and taking over the full mortgage yourself. Lenders may not allow you to take on the full mortgage if they do not believe you are capable of meeting the repayments.

- Handing over the home to one partner. This will only happen in very rare cases, for instance if your husband has far greater resources than you and you clearly have a much greater need for the home.

Staying put

If you want to stay in the family home, speak to your lender as soon as possible about what arrangements will be made for paying the mortgage. Bear in mind if you have a joint mortgage, you are liable for the full payments yourself if your ex-husband will not pay up. If your mortgage is in arrears, try to reach an agreement with your lender as soon as possible to avoid repossession.

Your income

It is obviously very important to get as much income as you can for yourself and your children, especially if you have not been working outside the home.

- You may be able to reach an agreement with your partner over how much maintenance he should pay you, or you can apply to the court for a maintenance order.
- If you are separated from your husband but not yet divorced and you are on Income Support, he must pay you maintenance at risk of being prosecuted. But this liability ends when you divorce.
- As soon as you separate, find out whether you are entitled to any social security benefits. One Parent Benefit is no longer available to new claimants. It is effectively being phased out.

Tax matters

Your tax situation will change as a result of divorce, so it is important to notify your tax office.

- It is most likely that your ex-husband was getting the Married Couples' Allowance. If so, he will continue to receive it until the end of the tax year in which you split up. If you were receiving all or part of the allowance, you will also continue to receive it until the end of the tax year in which you split up.
- You can claim an Additional Personal Allowance if you are bringing up a child or children on your own. You can continue to claim so long as you have a child under 16, even if you live with a new partner, but you lose the allowance if you remarry. It has the same cash value as the Married Couple's Allowance. If you are not a taxpayer, however, you cannot claim this or any other tax relief.
- If both of you buy a new home, you are both entitled to Mortgage Interest Relief at Source or MIRAS on the interest on the first £30,000 of the loan.
- You do not have to pay tax on any maintenance payments your ex-husband makes to you, unless they fall under 'old rules' abolished in the Finance Act 1988.

Child support

The controversial Child Support Agency was set up to deal with the problem of 'absent parents' (usually fathers) who do not pay proper maintenance for their children. Any single mother, whether she was married or not, can apply to the CSA for a maintenance assessment against the 'absent parent'.

Single mothers who are receiving means-tested benefits such as Income Support or Family Credit must apply to the CSA for a maintenance assessment, unless doing so would cause 'harm or undue distress', for example if your ex-husband is violent.

If you refuse to co-operate for any other reason, your benefits will be reduced.

If they can afford it, single mothers should make sure they have sufficient life insurance to look after their children in case anything happens. Few single mothers will be able to purchase many insurance products, however, no matter how essential your insurance seller claims them to be.

Money management

The old social stereotype of the man taking sole control of the family finances is dying out. But some women still find themselves being forced to handle money for the first time when they divorce. And even though married women typically take care of day-to-day household finances, research has shown that men still dominate major money decisions, and that many women continue to find finance intimidating.

Don't be afraid to ask for help and advice from your bank or mortgage lender.

If you have received a lump sum settlement from your ex-husband, it is important to make the best use of it. Seek independent financial advice. On divorce, you will have to unravel your joint finances. Tell your bank or building society to freeze any joint accounts and set up new ones in your own name.

Normally the proceeds are split half and half, unless you and your ex-husband specify otherwise. If you have run up any joint debts, you may be liable for the full amount if your husband defaults. See Chapters 6 and 7 for more details.

On divorce, you will want to make a new will to reflect your changed circumstances. Divorce does not completely cancel a will but can cause serious complications, so it is vital to make a new one.

More information

The Solicitors' Family Law Association has a database of members:

PO Box 302
Orpington
BR6 8QX
Tel: 01689 850227

The Consumers' Association publishes an excellent book, The *Which? Guide to Divorce*, available from the Which? Bookshop, 359–361 Euston Road, London NW1, or tel: 0800 252100.

Relate (National Marriage Guidance),
Herbert Gray College
Little Church Street
Rugby
CV21 3AP
Tel: 01788 573241

National Council for One Parent Families
255 Kentish Town Road
Kentish Town
London NW5 2LX
Tel: 0171-267 1361

Child Support Agency Helpline, tel: 0345 133133. Calls are charged at local rates.

The Inland Revenue publishes some helpful leaflets, available from tax offices: IR92, *Tax — A Guide for One Parent Families*, and IR 93, *Separation, Divorce and Maintenance Payments*. See also leaflet NI 95, *National Insurance for Divorced Women*, available from Benefits Agencies.

22
Charitable giving

This book has so far been concerned about how you can help yourself to a more secure financial future. Depending on who you are, your age and your position in life, that can mean anything from making the best use of the social security system to investing your spare money on the stockmarket. For many women, financial happiness comes from mixing and matching the many money strands that are faced over a normal life.

But this last chapter is different. It assumes you have read the previous sections and you have achieved a measure of financial well-being. No one can hope for more. Total security is an unattainable dream — and who is to define it anyway? You can be as unhappy with a million pounds as you can be happy with a thousand.

Provided you have achieved a degree of financial health, it could be time to think about giving some money away to good causes. There are literally tens of thousands of registered charities in the United Kingdom, although few donors will approve of all, let alone be in a position to give to more than a handful.

Charitable giving sounds easy once you have selected the cause. All you have to do is to put some cash into a collecting tin or send off a cheque or a credit card number to the organization you want to help. So it is fair to ask why charitable donations should appear as a subject in a Woman's Guide to Finance. The answer, and the point of this chapter, is to show that whatever you can afford to spare can be worth much more to the cause you choose if you give the money via one of the many tax relief routes which are detailed later in this chapter.

If you can put aside £1 a week, the £52 you amass over a year will be worth £52 to a charity if you use a collecting tin or send a cheque. But as long as you are a taxpayer, that same amount could be worth £67.53 to the good cause if you turn your gift into a tax deductible charitable donation. The charity receives the tax relief, so whatever you give is boosted by the Government. If you are a top rate taxpayer, the help from the state is even greater.

Charities are not just competing one with the other for what you can afford. They also face other calls on your money such as the National Lottery, where only a small proportion of the cash goes to good causes, and the growing necessity of having to prepare for retirement and old age through you own resources rather than relying on the state. Women feel this acutely. Later marriage and child-rearing, plus high divorce rates, create demographic factors which make generosity more difficult. Most large donors do so via a tax relief route. But if all the money given in other ways was to be diverted to this legal 'tax haven', charities would have tens of millions more a year to spend.

But charities also recognise that many women either cannot afford to help them, or would like to aid them with even more than they can send. No one is suggesting you run up an expensive overdraft. You can, however, help your favourite cause every time you shop by using an 'affinity card'. These are credit cards where a percentage of everything you buy with them goes to the cause pictured on the card, although the charity does not receive anything from interest or penalty payments.

There are over 200 affinity cards boosting everything from international aid charities to local football teams. So you can shop till your drop with a conscience! Virtually all stores accept credit cards, although John Lewis and Marks & Spencer are notable exceptions. Leaving those two groups aside, you can use an affinity card everywhere from food to petrol and via designer frocks. According to Womankind Worldwide, a charity that helps with women's issues in the developing world and which has just launched an affinity card, using their plastic could help turn shopping into a guilt-free experience!

Spending £1,000 on clothes — a spring, summer and autumn outfit perhaps — produces enough for Womankind to buy a milking goat and two chickens in Africa or to pay for a female worker to accompany a rape survivor to the nearest town's womens police station in Latin America to report the act of violence. Add the household necessities: holidays, car insurance and the hundreds of other expenditure items that can be put on a card, and the helping of others can increase dramatically.

Womankind Worldwide was started some nine years ago when Alec Reed of Reed Employment realised that 90 per cent of the aid going abroad ended up in male hands, while 90 per cent of the work was carried out by women, whose slow progress towards equality makes the problems of women in Europe and North America pale into insignificance. Its prime aim is to find groups in its target areas that fight abuse, over-

"The struggle for women's equality is part of the struggle for a better world for all human beings, and all societies"

UN SECRETARY GENERAL

WOMANKIND Worldwide is the UK's leading charity supporting Third World women in their fight against poverty and sexual or political oppression
Please remember us in your will and help to realise these women's dreams of a better future themselves their families and the whole of society
Ask for our booklet "Have You The Will" today - you can make a world of difference.
WOMANKIND Worldwide, 3 Albion Place, Galena Road, London W6 OLT
Tel: 0181 563 8608 Fax: 0181 563 8611   E-Mail: womankind@gn.apc.org
Web: http://www.oneworld.org/womankind

population and poverty rather than send money directly to alleviate problems. It has helped provide small credit amounts to female 'micro-entrepreneurs' in northern Ghana, train women as literacy teachers in Nicaragua, and provide awareness training for women ahead of local elections in Tamil Nadu state, India.

The fast growing charity should benefit from the new Millennium Gift Aid provisions which reduce the minimum level for a one off tax saving charitable donation from £250 to £100, provided the cause is involved with development issues in poorer countries abroad. It also raises money through 'givers' circles' where groups of women pledge to raise £1,000 or more between them to fund projects of particular interest to them.

The affinity card is a win-win situation. The charity benefits while you pay exactly the same for the goods you buy. So you are helping others at no extra cost to yourself. When you sign up for a card — Womankind Worldwide's affinity plastic is backed by the Bank of Scotland as are scores of other charity helping cards — your credit background will be checked as you will only receive the card if the bank thinks you can repay what you spend without too much trouble. If you already have a credit card, and have been operating the account without a problem, you should have no difficulty in passing the credit score test.

Once you use your activated card, the charity receives a lump sum — usually £5 or £10. After that, the card company hands over £2.50 for each £1,000 you spend. While that is not large, it is money that would otherwise have ended up in the credit card company's coffers.

Giving to charity may not rank as an investment in the ordinary sense, but it can be regarded as an investment in the future of society. Moreover, with a little organization — as opposed to simply giving to street collectors — it can be tax efficient.

The simplest arrangement is a payroll scheme, operated by an employer. This allows employees to make gifts directly from their salary, of up to £100 a month. The money is deducted before tax and paid to an approved Agency Charity with which the employer has an agreement. The employees, however, have a free choice of which charities their money goes to and the Agency Charity simply passes it on, although it may make a small charge for administration.

If your employer does not offer a payroll scheme, or you would like to make larger, one-off gifts, you can use Gift Aid. This carries a minimum for each gift of £250, net of basic rate tax, but there is no maximum. You give the charity a certificate which allows it to claim back basic rate tax from the Inland Revenue and, if you are a higher rate taxpayer, you may claim the extra 15 per cent. The Millennium Gift Aid scheme works on a similar basis with a minimum of £100. Only charities with approved projects in poorer countries will qualify.

The Charities Aid Foundation offers 'Personal Charity Accounts' for those giving through Gift Aid or covenants. The Foundation can reclaim tax on the gifts and also provides a 'cheque book' of vouchers which you can make out to your chosen charities.

Further information on Gift Aid is given in the Inland Revenue leaflet IR113 and from the Gift Aid helpline on 0151 472 6038. The Charities Aid Foundation can be contacted on 01732 771333.

Making an investment in a worthy cause

Vicki Pulman
Charities Aid Foundation

Giving to charity may not rank as an investment in the ordinary sense, but it can be regarded as an investment in the future of society. Moreover, with a little organisation it can be tax efficient.

Around 80 per cent of people in the UK make donations to charity. Few, however, are even aware of the full benefits available through the tax system, not just to the charities they choose to support, but to themselves. Overall, the Government has introduced three schemes for tax-effective giving, enabling both private individuals and corporate donors to make their charitable giving more effective.

A brighter future - with Intermediate Technology

When the news is so often dominated by disasters – wars and earthquakes, poverty and famine – it is all too easy to lose hope of any improvement. Yet there are millions of everyday successes achieved by poor people who are working to improve conditions for themselves and their families.

Often their efforts are hampered by a lack of suitable technologies – tools, equipment or know-how. This is where Intermediate Technology (IT) comes in, by helping to develop or introduce technologies that are matched to the skills, needs and resources of those who use them.

> 'When the starving of the world are pulled back from the brink of death with food aid the real problems still lie ahead and in this area Intermediate Technology is blazing a trail of hope...'
>
> **Sunday Times**

Training and the transfer of technical knowledge are at the heart of IT's approach. In poor rural communities of Africa, Asia and South America, IT works alongside local people, exploring with them the root causes of their problems and helping them to develop practical, long-term solutions.

> 'IT helped us to realise that we could do something for ourselves. In Keyo, we work as a group, we join hands, complete our work, then we go and help someone else.'
>
> *Florida Ogado, Keyo Women's Group, Kenya*

IT was established in 1966 by Dr Fritz Schumacher, author of the best-selling work *Small is Beautiful*.

This vital work depends on the generous support of IT's donors. To find out how you can help - through a covenant, or by remembering us in your will - please contact Winifred Dalby at:

> 'Since its foundation Intermediate Technology – of which I was proud to become the Patron in 1980 – has worked quietly and effectively, to the benefit of countless thousands of people. I commend its work and wish it continuing success in the future.'
>
> HRH The Prince of Wales

Intermediate Technology,
Myson House, Railway Terrace,
RUGBY, Warwickshire CV21 3HT.
Tel: (01788) 560631 Fax: (01788) 540270

Intermediate Technology Development Group Ltd. Patron: HRH The Prince of Wales, KG, KT, GCB. Company Registration No. 871954 England. Registered Charity No. 247257

Making an Investment in a Worthy Cause

Good investments are vital to secure a financial future for any woman and her family. We are wise to consider the expert advice we offered. but once these decisions hav ebeen made we can also invest in the future of the global family.

In the Third World it is inevitably the women who bear the hardest work load and the chief responsibility for the family - cooking, feeding children, collecting water and fuelwood, growing food for survival or for sale, and if opportubity permits, finding other work to supplement the family income. Their "investment" is time, hard work and traditional skills - to which the development charity Intermediate Technology adds training and technologies that are appropriate to people's needs.

The Keyo Women's Group in Western Kenya is a case in point. They, like other groups in the area, have proved that the above combination can lead to success in the form of a product which has had significant effects on the wellbeing of their families.

The product is an improved cooking stove, which has helped solve several problems at once. The traditional method of cooking on a three-stone fire, widely used throughout the Third World, has several disadvantages; three large stones are arranged in a circle, a pot is balanced precariously on top, and fuelwood is pushed in to the centre from all angles.

Not only is this an inefficient use of fuel: potential hazards are flying sparks, accidental burns from unstable pots, and - if used inside their house - the emission of harmful smoke, affecting the health of women and children. It is estimated that cooking on a three-stone fire in an unventilated kitchen is the equivalent of smoking 200 cigarettes a day!

One answer to this problem is the Upesi, an improved stove developed by Intermediate Technology. The Upesi, which means fast in Swahili, is a ceramic/pottery cylinder built into a mud surround in the kitchen. Several members of the Keyo Women's Group were already experienced potters, whose livelihoods had been threatened by the introduction of imported metal and plastic containers, and others received training.

The Upesi is designed to burn wood, although it can burn other types of "biomass" such as crop waste and maize stalks. It produces less smoke than the traditional open fire because it burns fuel more effectively. Also less fuel is needed so women spend less time collecting it. Health benefits shown by a study of 200 households using the Upesi stove were a reduction in acute respiratory diseases and conjunctivitis of between 60 - 70 per cent.

Making a Living

From simply producing and dinstalling the stoves for themselves, serveral women's groups have gone on to market them, either through stoves promoters at other outlets (such as a supermarket and even a Bata shoe shop!) or by giving demonstrations in the local market place on how to make and instal Upesis.

The stoves project is just one of many examples throughout the world where **Intermediate Technology** is combining its expertise with people's traditional skills, helping tham to work their way out of poverty. A donation or legacy to support this work could be your investment in the future of the global family.

Installing an Upesi Stove: marketplace demonstration

Donations made from taxed funds through any one of these schemes enables the Inland Revenue to repay the basic rate tax of around 25 per cent to the charity. If you are a higher rate taxpayer, you may reclaim the marginal rate of 15 per cent.

The schemes offer three very different methods of payment. These are by deed of covenant, payroll giving and Gift Aid. The *deed of covenant* is the oldest of the three and involves a contractual obligation to make regular donations over a period of four or more years. These payments can be made annually, monthly or in a lump sum, allowing the charity to subtract regular payments on its own behalf. Whichever method is used, tax is reclaimed and added to the total donation, increasing it by roughly one-third, at no extra cost to either you or the charity. There is no maximum amount payable under this scheme, although in order to cover the cost of administration, some charities may require a minimum donation.

Payroll giving was introduced by the government to encourage ongoing and regular gifts to charity. Since 1987, this scheme has enabled donors paying PAYE to make monthly contributions direct from their pay or pension at source, before tax is levied. The donor then pays tax at the usual rate but only on its remaining income. A donation, for example, of £50 per month made from pre-taxed income, would cost you £37.50 in real terms and only £30 if you are a higher rate taxpayer. The maximum payable through this scheme is now £1200 per annum or £100 per month and the real benefit, particularly to the charity, is in providing it with a regular source of income with which to budget and plan ahead.

Gift Aid is the most recent scheme and was introduced in 1991. It is the only scheme allowing single, one-off donations to be made tax effectively. In order to qualify, the gift has to amount to at least £250 but there is no obligation to repeat the donation. As with the covenant, however, tax is reclaimed by the charity at basic rate. This increases the minimum gift of £250 to £333.33 and allows higher rate donors to reclaim the marginal rate of around £50 for themselves.

Donkeys in the Third World play a vital role in the economy. As draught animals they are imperative to the survival of the impoverished farmer and his family. Without the donkey to carry their loads from the fields, their firewood and their water, life would be unbearable.

A donkey is as important in the Third World as a car is to the family in the Western World but, despite its importance, the donkey has little status and is abused and generally neglected.

We wish to put an end to the unnecessary suffering of donkeys but we are not opposed to them being worked humanely. The use of donkeys in the Third World countries enables the culture of the area to remain intact. Mechanisation is not only responsible for polluting and damaging the environment but, in under developed countries, is often too costly to maintain. The donkey has been a beast of burden for centuries and our aim is to raise its status, to prevent cruelty and to promote kindness to donkeys.

Please can you help us in our work. We employ vets and farriers from the countries where we work and are very cost effective.

There is one condition when making donations through any tax-effective scheme: the money has to go to a charity either registered with the Charity Commission or recognised by the Inland Revenue as being charitable. Organisations such as scout groups, places of worship, schools and hospitals, while not being registered charities, are all considered to be 'charitable'. Despite the obvious benefits of these schemes, for many they lack the flexibility and the spontaneity essential when giving to charity. There is a way, however, in which you can respond to a radio or television appeal, send off a few pounds in response to an advertisement or even give to a local street collector – tax effectively.

A personal charity account scheme, operated by an agency such as the Charities Aid Foundation (CAF), enables you to pay your tax-efficient donation into an account rather than direct to a single charity. As a registered charity itself, CAF reclaims the basic rate tax on the donor's behalf and adds it to the amount already in the account, deducting a small administrative contribution. So, on an initial payment of, say, £120, a revised balance of £152 is created at no extra cost to you. Higher rate taxpayers would be able to reclaim a further £24 for themselves.

Once the money is in the account, you are issued with a voucher book, similar to a cheque book, and a CAF Charity Card, a debit card designed specifically for charitable giving. This helps you to support any charity or cause of your choice and in whatever amounts, either by writing out a voucher in the charity's name or by giving the charity your card details.

Where would your donation go? Take, for example, the balance of £152 used above (which has cost the higher rate taxpayer only £96): £10 could be used to support a local community group, £50 could go to a place of worship, another £50 could go to an international aid agency and the balance perhaps to a local hospice. It is entirely your choice.

An added advantage to using an account is that CAF will honour only those donations made to registered or recognised

PLEASE HELP US TO HELP THEM

Mozart was confined alone in a stable for 2¹/₂ years. He was visited only occasionally to be brought food and water. His bed was a build up of his own dung. Mozart's hooves had grown long and twisted, he had lice and was in terrible pain.

When we rescued him he was petrified. He would cower at the back of his new stable when approached. When the door was opened it was many days before Mozart ventured out and he was just as frightened of donkeys as he was of people.

Gradually, with patience and kindness, Mozart is beginning to trust again.

Over 7,600 donkeys have been taken into our care, many from lives of cruelty and neglect. To continue our work, we really need your help - either by direct donation or a legacy.

Please send donations to: The Donkey Sanctuary (Dept. WGF98),
Sidmouth, Devon, EX10 ONU, Tel: (01395) 578222. Fax: (01395) 579266
Registered Charity Number 264818

Over 7,600 donkeys have been taken into care, many from lives tormented by cruelty and neglect. A donkey is never turned away from our Sanctuary and never put down unless there is no longer any quality of life. We need your help to continue rescuing donkeys and to provide them with a home where they can spend their remaining days grazing peacefully and receiving loving care.

Any donation, no matter the amount is greatly appreciated and our doners' list is carefully guarded - we never release details to other organizations.

Administration costs are kept to a minimum - just 7.4p in the £1.

If you would like to receive further information, including a copy of our "Will Making Guide", please do not hesitate to contact us. A legacy is of great value to us in ensuring the future of our large donkey family - many of the donkeys live to 40/50+ years. In return we remember with deep gratitude those who have left us a bequest by inscribing their names on our Memory Wall and remembering them at out Memorial Service held every year on The Feast Day of St. Francis of Assisi.

Please send donations to: The Donkey Sanctuary, (Dept. WGF98),
Sidmouth, Devon, EX10 ONU. Tel: (01395) 578222. Fax: (01395) 579266
Administrator and Founder Dr. Elisabeth D. Svendsen, M.B.E.

charities, thereby protecting the money from going to an organisation which is not bona fide.

If you have slightly larger amounts to distribute – a bequest under a will or investments that you wish to give to a charity free of capital gains tax – setting up a charitable trust may be an ideal solution. It can provide enduring support for charities and causes even beyond your lifetime and can help to develop close links with those supported on a regular basis.

Before pursuing this option, however, it needs to be given careful consideration. First, there are legal and accountancy fees to be considered. Trustees need to be taken on, decisions taken over trust fund investment and accounting, separate bank accounts need to be opened and annual reports, returns and accounts all need to be submitted to the Charity Commission. It can take anything from 6 to 12 months simply to get the trust up and running.

By using an agency such as the Charities Aid Foundation, a trust can be established almost immediately and, coming under the guardianship of CAF's own trustees, there is no need to appoint them independently. Another advantage is that there are usually no initial fees or legal charges and CAF will take care of all administration requirements on behalf of the trust holder. Initially, all that is required of the donor is a sum of at least £10,000 – £7,700 plus tax reclaimed (or the commitment to reach that level within two or three years) – a name for the trust which, within reason, is up to the donor and a decision on the duration of the trust.

Once the trust has been established, it operates rather like a bank account. The capital is invested by CAF although the emphasis, such as high income or capital growth, is chosen by the trust holder.

The three investment funds operated by CAF are the Balanced Growth Fund, providing sustained capital growth and increasing growth of income, the Income Fund, which maximises income return with an element of capital protection, and the CAF Cash Deposit Fund, which pools investments to create a high rate of interest. The three schemes are designed exclusively for charities and trusts in a tax-effective way and are used by thousands of such organisations.

As with tax-effective giving, when it comes to distributing funds from the trust, donations may only be made to registered or recognised charities either by using a voucher book. or standing order. Capital can be added to the trust at any time, and tax effectively, and all rights and responsibilities of the trust can be passed on at any time to a successor of the trust holder's choosing.

Under the current schemes, it has never been easier to support the charities of your choice tax effectively, whether you give in a sustained and regular way, make your donations spontaneously and with flexibility, or whether you simply want to ensure that both you and the charities you support gain the maximum benefit from your donations.

Further information on Gift Aid is given in the Inland Revenue leaflet IR113 and on the Gift Aid helpline on 0151 472 6038.

For further information about the Charities Aid Foundation's Charity Account Scheme telephone 01732 771333; or to find out more about the trust service contact 01892 512244.

Payroll giving and voucher accounts

With a cache of money to dispense or save as you please you may wish to consider opportunities to give regularly to charity either as and when you like or through your salary. Payroll giving is a tax-free way to give from your pay. The voucher account system offers a versatile and flexible way to give to charity. Both schemes are administered by the Charities Trust.

Charities Trust is incorporated and registered as a charitable company to operate as a payroll giving agency in accordance with Sections 505 and 506 of the Income and Corporation Taxes Act 1988. Charities Trust aims to provide a high quality payroll giving service, which is non-profit making. The trust acts as a clearing house, sending donations to the chosen charities. Money is taken directly from the donor's pay with the benefit of tax relief. Any one of a quarter of a million causes can benefit. All contributions have to be distributed within 80 days of receipt and the interest obtained on deposit during that time helps to offset costs.

The administration fee is designed to cover the cost of the processing of the donor's requirements and the distribution to the selected charities. The fee is currently 5 per cent or 30p per donor per month, whichever is the greater. The breakdown of a single donation of £10 would be as follows: agency charge of 50p, cost to taxpayer of £7.50, charity receives £9.50.

How the payroll giving system works

A maximum of four charities per person is permitted. The minimum donation per charity is 25p per week or £1 per month. Donors can vary their choice of charity or stop giving at any time. A statement of donations can be provided to employers on request at the end of each tax year.

Employers provide to employees a facility for a pre-tax deduction for charitable donations. Employers send those donations to Charities Trust monthly together with a list of donors. It is recommended that the donor code used is the employer's payroll number or National Insurance number. Donations are sent before the 19th of the following month in line with PAYE.

Employers should note that to achieve maximum tax benefits, they need to enter into a contract with an Agency Charity and register with the Inland Revenue. Charities Trust can undertake this on their behalf. Donors leaving a company's employment are entitled to request from the employer a statement of their contributions made during the tax year.

Employers may elect to match employee donations and/or pay their administration fees. To ease administration, personnel departments are advised to produce easy-to-follow forms to input for submission to Charities Trust and use constant donor/employee reference numbers. Inland Revenue

LEAVE A LEGACY OF CONSTANT COMPANIONSHIP

The comfort and companionship of a radio means the world to someone who is blind and living alone. The British Wireless for the Blind Fund provides special audio equipment on free lifelong loan to UK-registered blind people who cannot afford to buy their own.

Legacies are crucial to the future of our work.

If you are considering a charitable bequest, please remember the British Wireless for the Blind Fund. For further information about our work, contact:

BRITISH WIRELESS FOR THE BLIND FUND
Gabriel House, 34 New Road, Chatham, Kent ME4 4QR.
Tel: (01634) 832501. Fax:(01634) 817485. Reg.Charity No: 211849

THE BRITISH WIRELESS FOR THE BLIND FUND
1928 -1998 - Seventy Years of caring for blind people in need

The British Wireless for the Blind Fund was established in 1928 to provide the companionship of radio to every blind person in the country who is in need.

In our Seventieth Anniversary Year, the Fund's aim hasn't changed in the least, but the challenge has become greater than ever.

There are currently over 181,000 people in Britain who are registered blind. Each year around 14,000 names are added to the UK register.

Nearly half of all registered blind people live alone. Many live on a very limited income - and the cost of a dependable radio is often more than they can afford.

The British Wireless for the Blind Fund strives to meet a growing demand - both for audio equipment and for the provision of service.

Our range of radios, radio-cassette recorders and TV sound receivers are provided on free permanent loan for life to UK-registered blind people in need. We also undertake to maintain, repair or replace equipment whenever necessary.

Today there are more than 70,000 sets provided by the Fund in use around the country. Since 1928 the Fund has provided more than three quarters of a million radios to registered blind people who cannot afford to buy their own.

The British Wireless for the Blind Fund is an independent charity. We rely on private donations, covenants and especially legacies to carry on our work.

Full details about the Fund are available from: The British Wireless for the Blind Fund, Gabriel House, 34 New Road, Chatham, Kent ME4 4QR.

Tel:(01634) 832501 Fax:(01634) 817485 E-mail:Lin@blind.org.uk Reg. Charity No: 211849

regulations prohibit the return of any money withheld from employees.

Voucher accounts

Alternatively, you can open a voucher account. The minimum monthly donation is £120 per annum – £10 per month. The maximum individual donation is £1200 per annum. With the tax advantage, a £10 donation would cost only £7.70. The scheme gives you the flexibility to give to whomever you want, whenever you want.

The money is paid into a 'pot' and whenever you wish to make a donation, whether it be to the local hospice or a TV extravaganza, the money is paid out. A book of vouchers or a charity cheque book is issued to you to enable this to happen.

A group voucher scheme runs alongside the individual voucher scheme. A 'group' is considered a minimum of five individuals. These contribute to a 'pot'. The minimum and maximum donations by the group are the same as for the individual's scheme: £120 and £1200 per annum respectively. One employee is nominated to complete and return a group voucher account registration form to Charities Trust. An account number will then be issued.

In addition, each employee donating to the group completes a Charity Choice Form but nominates the group account number rather than a specific charity. Once the group or individual account is established, a book of vouchers will be supplied.

The vouchers are completed at the individual's discretion like a cheque book and forwarded to the charity. The charity will complete its section and return the voucher to Charities Trust for processing. Please remember that the charity must be or become registered with Charities Trust. A statement of account is provided on a quarterly basis to the account holder(s). Statements show donations made (less an administration charge of 5 per cent maximum), vouchers issued and balance available to use.

Charities Trust can also offer personal advice to companies on how employers can save time and money, how voucher

accounts can be set up, enabling irregular donations to be made to an assortment of charities. The trust is the second largest payroll giving agency in the United Kingdom. It currently handles over 800 employers and more than 100,000 donors. Funds are distributed to over 2,000 charities.

For further information contact: Charities Trust, PO Box 15, Liverpool L23 0UU. Telephone: 0151 949 0044.

Wills, legacies and charitable giving

Making wills is an age-old occupation. It is quite impossible to say when the first will was made, by whom and under what circumstances. There are of course copies of ancient wills still in existence or records of what they contain. The purpose of wills has, however, never changed as it represents the inalienable right of people to leave their lifetime possessions to whomsoever they wish. For some it also provides an opportunity to speak from beyond the grave and throughout history all manner of people have used their wills to express unflattering observations about their kith and kin. Equally, some of the sentiments expressed in wills about friends, relatives and reasons for leaving money to charity are loving and heart warming and depict the best features of human nature.

The style and nature of wills has of course changed down the centuries. Here is an example of a will by Joshua West of the Six Clerks' Office in Chancery Lane, made in the eighteenth century. He wrote:

Perhaps I died not worth a groat;
but should I die worth something more,
then I give that, and my best coat,
and all my manuscripts in store, to those
who shall the goodness have
to cause my poor remains to rest
within a decent shell and grave.
This is the Will of Joshua West.

With the passage of time the collection and storage of wills became more regularised and a system evolved whereby probate matters in England and Wales were dealt with by a mixture of almost 400 ecclesiastical and secular courts. Some of these, including the Prerogative Court of the Archbishop of Canterbury, were situated at the famous Doctors Commons near St Paul's Cathedral and it was there that the Principal Probate Registry was first located.

In 1857 Parliament passed The Court of Probate Act which established the Principal Probate Registry and 40 District Probate Registries in England and Wales with effect from 12 January 1858. In October 1874 the great collection of wills stored in old Doctors Commons was transported through the streets of London in vans and wagons to Somerset House in the Strand into offices vacated by the Admiralty in the previous year. One hundred and twenty three years on, Somerset House remains the central repository for wills proved in England and Wales.

The case for challenging a will

In most respects the law in England and Wales provides the greatest freedom of choice for will makers in comparison with other countries. In other words, anyone from the age of 18 onwards can make a will disposing of their worldly goods in any way they choose. This of course can and does lead to injustices and where this occurs claimants have a right to challenge the will under the Inheritance (Provision for Families and Dependants) Act 1975. The basis of any claim is failure by the deceased to make reasonable financial provision for any person or persons who had some degree of financial dependence upon them prior to death. In other words, the plaintiff can claim compensation for the loss of benefit out of the estate.

The legal position is that claims should be made within six months from the date of grant of representation (probate) but the court can extend this time limit in very special circumstances. In order for the Act to be applied the deceased must have died domiciled in England and Wales. Currently the classes of persons who may challenge a will under the 1975 Act are:

- wife or husband of deceased;
- former wives or husbands of deceased who have not remarried;
- a child of the deceased;
- any person (not being a child of the deceased) who, in the case of any marriage to which the deceased was at any time a party, was treated by the deceased as a child of the family in relation to the marriage;
- any person (other than those above) who immediately before the death of the deceased was being maintained, either wholly or partly, by the deceased;
- for deaths on or after 1 January 1996, a new category: persons living with the deceased in the same household and as the husband or wife of the deceased, during the two years immediately prior to the date of death (Law Reform (Succession) Act 1995).

The first Act of this kind was introduced in the 1930s since prior to that date a will in England and Wales could only be challenged on the basis that the legator was not of testamentary capacity – in other words they were not considered to be of sound mind, memory and understanding. This was a very unsatisfactory state of affairs since in order to gain redress for any injustice created by the will the plaintiff could only in effect allege that the deceased was of unsound mind. This could be deeply distressing when the testator or testatrix was a loved relative. It still remains a fact that wills are occasionally contested on the basis that the deceased did not have testamentary capacity, but in most cases wills are now challenged under the 1975 Act.

In Scotland the position is markedly different. Under Scottish law a will can be challenged on a number of grounds – for example if the person were insane when it was made, if children were born after the will was made, if the person had been improperly influenced by another person when making the will. The 1975 Act referred to earlier does not apply to Scotland in that there are inbuilt rights to protect the immediate family. Basically, what-

Please remember that animals need your help and support

Since 1926 UFAW has been working at home and abroad to improve conditions for animals in zoos, in laboratories, on farms, in the home and the wild.

UFAW is a science-based animal welfare charity which gives research grants, provides advice and publishes information on improving animal care. It is an independent charity and does not receive income from universities, commerce or government.

With your help we can continue this important work - please remember UFAW in your Will.

Universities Federation for Animal Welfare
The Old School, Brewhouse Hill,
Wheathampstead, Herts AL4 8AN
Tel: 01582 831818

Registered Charity No. 207996

ever the will says, a surviving husband, wife or children can if they wish, after 'prior rights' have been satisfied, claim further 'legal rights' to a proportion of any property excluding house and land.

The amounts designated under 'prior rights' are changed from time to time but the current provision is as follows.

Prior rights

These are the surviving husband's or wife's rights to (a) the house (up to the value of £110,000); (b) furniture in the house (up to £20,000); (c) a payment of £30,000 if there are children, £50,000 if there are not.

Legal rights

After prior rights have been dealt with, a surviving husband or wife and children have certain 'legal rights' to a proportion of the 'moveable estate' – that is, all things such as money, shares, cars, furniture and jewellery.

Where there is an intestacy (no will) and any prior or legal rights have been dealt with, the remainder of the estate is given to surviving relatives according to a strictly laid-down sequence – for example, any children have first claim; if there are no children, half goes to the parents or parent and half to the brothers and sisters; if there are no children or parents, all goes to the brothers and sisters and so on. In the event of there being no qualifying relatives in the case of an intestacy, the estate will pass to the Crown.

Because of the complexities in the law relating to claims and contested wills, it is imperative that plaintiffs, defendants and lay (non professional) executors seek legal advice from qualified solicitors.

Having set out the ways and means by which disputes over wills can be resolved, it is important to remember that the overwhelming majority of wills create no problems at all and the intended beneficiaries receive their bequests as the will maker intended.

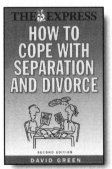

Why make a will?

Let us now consider the reasons why people make wills. As already stated, anyone over the age of 18 in England and Wales is eligible to make a will, whereas in Scotland girls from the age of 12 and boys from the age of 14 are able to make wills. Some people make a will at quite an early age, perhaps because they are involved in a dangerous job, pursuit or hobby or serving in Her Majesty's forces. Long-distance travel or going abroad as a family often motivates people to make a will. Another strong reason for making a will is marriage or partnership or buying a house. It is also very important for people to make a will when their children are born, both to provide financial security and deal with guardianship issues. Divorce does not totally invalidate a will except where it affects the provisions made for the former husband or wife. As life moves on, the marriage or partnership of children may motivate parents to make wills, as may the birth of grandchildren. The problems associated with the ageing process are often the main reasons for making wills such as illness, the death of loved ones and the general desire to put one's affairs in order. Experience of dealing with an intestacy is another strong motivator for making a will. Moral – don't make life harder for the loved ones you leave behind.

Above and beyond all else, it is important for people to realise that the only way to ensure their worldly possessions pass to the beneficiaries of their choice is to make a will. It is often presupposed that there is no need to make a will because the immediate family will benefit anyway, which is to some extent true where the estate is of modest size. In the case of high-value estates, it has been known for husbands or wives in particular to find that the provisions under the Intestacy Rules do not sufficiently cater for their needs and it may then be necessary in England and Wales to seek further and better provision under the 1975 Inheritance Act.

Tax considerations

For some people tax planning is important and anyone wishing to make special arrangements to reduce or avoid tax should

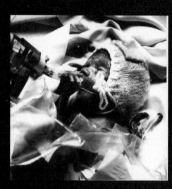

seek expert advice. Bequests to a surviving husband or wife are totally exempt from inheritance tax as are gifts through wills to charities. Other beneficiaries, such as children, are liable to pay tax on any inheritances they receive in excess of the inheritance tax threshold. With effect from 6 April 1998 the inheritance tax threshold was raised to £223,000 from the previous level of £215,000. This will clearly release quite a few more estates from tax completely. For estates over £223,000 a flat rate tax of 40 per cent is levied on the excess unless it passes to exempt beneficiaries as mentioned earlier.

There are other ways of reducing the burden of tax on estates but because of the unique nature of each person's affairs it is always advisable to obtain professional advice on the legitimate ways in which this can be done. While many solicitors have knowledge in this field, it is sometimes better to consult accountants who probably have the greatest skills in this area of tax planning.

At the moment, for instance, we have what is generally known as the seven-year rule. This relates to any personal gifts made during a person's lifetime in excess of the annual or other specific exemptions, such as gifts on marriage known as 'potentially exempt transfers'. These transfers are subject to inheritance tax only if the person who makes the gift dies within a seven-year period from the time of making the gift. Tax is reduced on a sliding scale depending on how many years have elapsed before the donor's death as shown below:

Years before death	Percentage of full tax charge
0–3	100
3–4	80
4–5	60
5–6	40
6–7	20

The wealth factor

It is impossible to say how many people place a high priority on tax planning when making their wills but, looking at the wealth statistics produced by Smee & Ford, the vast majority of people who die each year do not leave large estates. For instance, in 1994 there were approximately 544,000 adult deaths in England and Wales. Of these fewer than half (247,491) left estates worth over £5000. The probate value of these estates was £17.66 billion; 53,409 or 21.6 per cent died intestate, the cumulative value of their estates being £2.02 billion. The 194,082 will makers together left £15.64 billion. Furthermore, detailed analysis indicated that 85 per cent of the will makers had estates worth between £5000 and £125,000, suggesting that the great majority could be described as cash poor but asset rich. In other words, for most of them their house would have been their most valuable possession. Just under 15 per cent of will makers had estates valued between £125,000 and £1 million. People leaving estates in excess of £1 million totalled 690 or 0.4 per cent of all will makers. Fourteen millionaires died intestate and of course their estates would be distributed in accordance with the Intestacy Rules.

Professional involvement

Although available evidence indicates that relatively few will makers take financial advice from accountants when making their wills, it is very important that they consult a solicitor who will be able to give sound legal advice, particularly when complicated provisions are required. The research carried out by Smee & Ford reveals that the majority of will makers still appoint lay executors only but in most cases these executors engage solicitors to obtain the Grant of Probate and carry out the subsequent estate administration on their behalf. Many will makers appoint non-professional executors because they believe it will reduce the cost of administering their estates but, for the reasons stated above, legal charges are incurred by the employment of solicitors who will require a written undertaking from the lay executors that their proper professional fees will be deductible from the estate. When solicitors are themselves appointed executors their charging clause will automatically be written into the will. All the main banks provide a will making and probate service but have only a very tiny percentage of the executorship market, possibly due to the fact that their charges are for the most part higher than the fees charged by solicitors.

It is of course quite feasible for people to make home-made wills or use the standard forms which can be obtained from stationer's shops. Providing people observe the basic legal requirements, such wills are perfectly valid and raise no problems in implementation. Even so, the best advice is to consult a solicitor who will be prepared to give prospective clients a quote for making their will. The cost of a solicitor-made will is not nearly as high as some people believe. In some cases it can be less than £50 with special deals for joint wills made by husbands, wives or partners.

Legal requirements

The basic principles for making a valid will are that it must be in writing and must appoint executors. The attestation clause must follow the legal requirement that the testator and two witnesses be together and sign the will in the presence of each other. In the case of Scotland, only one witness is now required, but there the testator is required to sign each page of the will, whereas in England and Wales the testator need only sign the attestation clause on the final page along with the two witnesses. Although it is possible to have up to four executors, one is sufficient, but on balance it is preferable to choose two people such as a solicitor and a younger adult relative or close friend. Remember, a will may be declared invalid if it has not been signed and dated by the testator in the presence of the witness or witnesses who must also sign the will. Witnesses do not need to know the contents of the will they are witnessing nor should they be beneficiaries, since being a witness or a spouse of a witness could invalidate any gift bequeathed to them if the will is made in England and Wales. In Scotland it is preferable not to have the will witnessed by a beneficiary but this will not invalidate the attestation or (as in England and

Wales) the gift. On the other hand, an executor may be named as a beneficiary in any will.

As indicated earlier, the sole purpose of making a will is to dispose of one's lifetime possessions and to decide on the list of beneficiaries who are to inherit your estate. There are three main types of legacy. The first is a specific gift such as a car, house, item of jewellery or other household effect. If at the time of death the gift described in the will cannot be found or identified, it will fail. The second type of legacy is a pecuniary (cash) gift of any size (for example £1000). The third type of legacy is what is called a residuary bequest, which is all or part of the balance of the estate after all debts, taxes, expenses and other legacies have been paid. With the passage of time, pecuniary legacies will lose value because of inflation and legators may therefore wish either to index-link their cash gifts to family, friends and charity or divide the whole estate into shares or percentages so that all classes of beneficiaries will gain if the value of the estate increases between the will being made and the time of death.

Charitable giving through wills

Despite the growing incidence of divorce and the increasing numbers of people who live alone, the strong allegiance to family and other loved ones is still reflected in the provisions of wills, but there have always been a minority of legators who make charitable bequests. Although this amounts only to about one will maker in seven, Smee & Ford estimate that in England and Wales alone charitable will makers collectively leave £1 billion to their favourite causes each year. It is the second most productive form of voluntary income for charitable organisations and any diminution in this source of funding will have very serious implications for most of the United Kingdom's leading charities. To illustrate this point further, the following charities among many others receive over 50 per cent of their total voluntary income from legacies: RNLI, Imperial Cancer Research Fund, Cancer Research Campaign, Guide Dogs for the

Blind Association, Barnardo's, RNIB, Salvation Army, RSPCA and British Heart Foundation. A number of smaller charities are also heavily dependent upon legacy income including the Dogs' Home, Battersea which every year receives more than 90 per cent of its income in the form of legacies.

It may well be that far more people could be influenced into leaving charitable gifts, bearing in mind the tax benefits to both the giver and the receiver. Charities have been influential over the years in promoting the concept of will making since there is no provision for charities under the Intestacy Rules. No will equals no charitable bequest.

It is to be hoped that with the passage of time and continuing growth of individual wealth more people will see the wisdom of making a will and not allow the law to have the final say in their affairs. I began this article by quoting an ancient will and I will end with a few lines from a very recent will:

> O, grant me, heaven, a middle state,
> Neither too humble, nor too great,
> More than enough, for nature's ends,
> With something left to treat my friends.

Bernard Sharpe is Director of Consultancy with Smee & Ford Ltd, having previously worked in the charity sector for over 20 years, promoting and administering legacies for the RNLI and SCOPE.

Giving to charity – the cost-free way

Trudie Harris, Head of Communications, WOMANKIND Worldwide

Charitable donations from professional 30-something women have, just like most other age/social groups been steadily falling over the years, both in terms of frequency of donations, and overall value of donations. Why this is, few are sure – as with most phenomena it is highly unlikely to be due to just one factor. What can be said though is that with the average age for marriage increasing and the expectancy that your husband will 'provide for you' disappearing, women are having to 'look out for themselves', to put money aside for pensions, healthcare or their own mortgages.

But for many of us the charitable instinct is still there nonetheless. The public outpouring of grief after Diana, Princess of Wales' death manifested itself in a strong desire to do something to enable her charitable work to carry on. The result? A memorial fund that grew out of hundreds of thousands of donations from everyday people.

And it's not just the dramatic events like Diana's death that shock us into a wish to make a difference. Many of us care deeply about the 'newer' charity issues like the Environment, Human Rights or Breast Cancer. Whilst we may see our role increasingly as one of 'solidarity, not charity' we still recognise that part of that solidarity must mean giving money to help a cause.

The question then for many women is how can they contribute to good work without having it hit them hard financially. Well, at last there's a 'Win-Win' option that costs an individual nothing, but can make a huge difference to a charity. Sounds too good to be true? Enter the Affinity Credit Card.

We all now use credit cards increasingly often – a trip to the supermarket, petrol, a shopping spree – the flexible friend is there to lighten the financial load and facilitate good financial management. But did you know that just by swapping your airmiles or reward points credit card for one of the charity affinity cards – offered through the likes of Royal Bank of Scotland, the Co-operative Bank and US bank MBNA – you could be helping someone else at no extra cost to yourself?

One example is the new WOMANKIND Worldwide credit card, billed as the world's first 'guilt-free credit card for women'. Using this card, every time you shop 'til you drop, you could be dropping something into a global fund for third world women in their fight against poverty, and political or sexual oppression. From every guilt ridden bargain binge and manic sales spend can come the welcome comfort of knowing that in

Africa, India and Latin America groups of women will benefit. The more goods you put on the card, the more money the charity earns.

Many of the major British charities now have Affinity Credit Cards which their supporters, or the general public, can apply for. It's a simple, effective way to make a difference, and more importantly for those of us struggling to make ends meet – it costs us nothing whatsoever. Think about it: the value of the good work that you could be helping to fund is worth bearing in mind next time you get your loyalty 'Asparagus Poacher', or the like, from your traditional credit card company.

Appendix
More help and advice

Sources of further information and help are listed at the ends of the relevant chapters. There are, however, useful places to turn for general guidance.

General financial planning guidance

Most women will want to seek advice from a financial expert before making a major investment decision. Advisers fall into two categories: independent financial advisers who should recommend you the best product on the whole market, and tied agents or company representatives who can only offer you a product from their own company's range.

Always ask the adviser which sort he or she is. Most financial journalists and commentators believe it is better to go to an independent adviser.

You will not normally be asked to write a cheque to pay for the advice. But that doesn't mean it's free — advisers earn their living through commissions on anything they sell you.

Both sorts of adviser are paid by commission which is taken out of the money you invest. It means an adviser might be tempted to recommend you an unsuitable product just because it pays him a high commission, or to sell you something you don't need at all.

To avoid this and increase your chances of genuinely unbiased advice, you can go to an adviser who charges a fee.

Financial advisers and investment companies ought to be authorised by the appropriate regulator. For most of the firms you deal with, the regulator will be the Personal Investment Authority. You can check whether a firm is authorised to do business by ringing the Financial Services Authority Register on 0171-929 3652.

For a list of independent financial advisers in your area, contact: IFA Promotions, tel: 0117 971 1177.

You can get a list of fee-charging independent financial advisers from: The Money Management National Register of Independent Fee-based Advisers, c/o Matrix Data Ltd, Freepost 22 (SW1565), London W1E 7EZ, tel: 01272 769444.

Complaints

There are several independent ombudsmen you can turn to if you have a complaint and reach deadlock with the firm concerned. You must have exhausted the firm's own complaints procedures before the ombudsman can help.

All can order the firms to make you an award, up to a given ceiling, often £50,000 or £100,000.

The Banking Ombudsman
70 Gray's Inn Road
London WC1X 8NB
Tel: 0171-404 9944

The Building Societies Ombudsman
Mill Bank Tower
Mill Bank
London SW1P 4XS
Tel: 0171-931 0044

The Insurance Ombudsman Bureau
135 Park Street
London SE1 9EA
Tel: 0171 928 7600

The Occupational Pensions Advisory Service (OPAS) will deal with disputes about both company and personal pensions. If OPAS cannot sort it out, the problem may be referred to the Pensions Ombudsman.

OPAS
11 Belgrave Road
London SW1V 1RB
Tel: 0171-233 8080

The Pensions Ombudsman is at the same address.

The Personal Investment Authority Ombudsman can help with complaints against investment and pension providers, and can award compensation.
PIA Ombudsman
Hertsmere House
Hertsmere Road
London E14 4AB
Tel: 0171-538 8860

Solicitors' Complaints Bureau
Victoria Court
8 Dormer Place
Leamington Spa
Warwickshire CU32 5AE
Tel: 01926 820082

Investments

The lead regulator for investment firms is the Financial Authority Services (FSA). FSA delegates powers to a number of other watchdogs. It has replaced the Securities and Investment Board. The Personal Investment Authority is the controlling organisation for firms carrying out retail business with the public, and is the one you are most likely to come across. The Securities and Futures Authority regulates stockbrokers. All have independent arrangements for dealing with investor complaints that cannot be resolved with the firm concerned.

Financial Services Authority
25 The North Colonnade
Canary Wharf
London E14 5HS
Tel: 0171-676 1000

Personal Investment Authority
1 Canada Square
Canary Wharf
London E14 5AZ
Tel: 0171-538 8860

Securities & Futures Authority
The Cotton Centre
Cottons Lane
London SE1 2QB
Tel: 0171-378 9000

Compensation

The Investors' Compensation Scheme which will pay out if you lose money through an authorised investment firm which goes bust or is fraudulent. It will not pay out just because you buy an investment which performs badly leading to a loss.

The maximum payout is £48,000 — full protection for the first £30,000 you invest, and 90 per cent of the next £20,000.

In the extremely unlikely event of a building society going bust, there is a compensation scheme which will pay 90 per cent of the first £20,000 of savings.

If a bank goes under, you are covered for 75 per cent of the first £20,000 invested with it.

Investment-linked insurance products are covered by the Policyholders Protection Act. You will receive at least 90 per cent of the amount guaranteed when the company went bust.
The Investors' Compensation Scheme
Gavrelle House
2–14 Bunhill Row
London EC1Y 8RA
Tel: 0171-628 8820

Benefits

Look in local phone books under 'Benefits Agency' or 'Social Security'.

Index

Index of advertisers